# LORD TEACH US TO PRAY

LESSONS ON PRAYER

# LORD TEACH US TO PRAY

## LESSONS ON PRAYER

ED WHITE

COLLEGE PRESS PUBLISHING CO., Joplin, Missouri

Printed and Bound in the
United States of America


International Standard Book Number: 0-89900-347-8
Library of Congress Catalog Card Number: 89-81418

# CONTENTS

# INTRODUCTION

The moral values of any society have a way of following a descending path after a period of spiritual renewal. It has always been that way. Under kings Asa and Jehoshaphat the moral climate in Judah rose markedly. The people were led to make a renewed commitment to the Lord. But, after the death of Jehoshaphat, the people regressed rapidly. Soon they were back to their old practice of idol worship with all its attendant evils. It was the same old story that had been re-enacted over and over again during the period of the judges.

It has been much the same in the Christian era. After the "great awakening" in the United States, the morals of society in general were highly elevated. They did not, of course, reach the standards of moral purity prescribed by the Lord. But, in that atmosphere Christians flourished. They lived in moral excellence, and though the worldly people all around them did not always choose to imitate them, they did at least respect them.

As the moral climate in any society begins to deteriorate, unfortunately, Christians usually relax their standards. They are satisfied to live on a plane somewhat higher than the world's standards rather than aspiring to the pattern of holiness set by Jesus. Then as the standards of society fall lower and lower, the Christians become satisfied with less and less holiness. The result is that the lifestyle of the average professing Christian has less of moral purity about it than did the lifestyle of the average non-Christian of a generation or two earlier. At that point the church becomes a part of the problem instead of the solution to society's ills.

Consider our own American society. Two generations ago Billy Sunday was a powerful force in the molding of our nation's conscience. His influence, and that of like thinking people was such that a majority of the politicians of that day actually passed an amendment to the U.S. Constitution which forbade the production and sale of alcoholic beverages. Can you imagine such a thing today? Instead we have a moral climate which allows the destruction of innocent unborn children at the rate of two million per year. It has bred a national mentality that now considers it acceptable to allow children who are less than perfect mentally or physically to starve to death at the discretion of the parents and their doctor. Pornography has become an eight billion dollar a year industry. As a direct result of such mind pollution, the frequency of sexual abuse of children has multiplied until it is a national disgrace, and it is still rising. Homosexuality has bred an epidemic of A.I.D.S., and more than 30 other sexually transmitted diseases are currently devastating the people of this country. Yet there is no significant movement to turn people back to pure living. Instead, the movement is toward so-called "safe sex."

Statistics within the Christian community are little better than those in the general population. Divorce is as prevalent among Christians as it is outside the church. Church people are succumbing to the temptations to live like the world. Preachers are being caught and are confessing to sexual misconduct. Elders have been caught molesting children. Elders' wives have been known to leave them to run off with their lovers. The average church member is not shocked or offended by profanity, nudity and sex on television and in the movies. We are living in one of those times when apathy and worldliness within the church have made her a part of the problem rather than the solution to the ills of the world.

It is no wonder the Lord told Solomon that when calamity befell Israel, the proper course of action would be for *His people, those who professed allegiance to Him*, to humble themselves and pray, and seek His face, and *turn from their wicked ways* (italics mine).

Many have noted the need for spiritual renewal in America and Western society as a whole. Many have proclaimed the need to follow the advice of II Chronicles 7:14, but I'm afraid most Christians don't really know how to pray. If the conditions of apathy and worldliness in our churches are to change, we must humble ourselves before the Lord, and learn to pray as Jesus taught His disciples. That is the purpose of this study. We will look at the words of Jesus in regard to prayer with special emphasis on the model prayer as it is recorded in Matthew 6:9-13. Our desire will be to learn from His model all that our Lord intended.

Evidently the disciples of our Lord saw that one thing which made Jesus different from all other men was His relationship with the Father in heaven. Perhaps they also came to believe that an explanation for that relationship could be found in His prayer life. They knew that He sometimes got up a great while before daylight to go out to a private place to pray. They knew that He sometimes spent an entire night in prayer. They also knew they wanted to be like Him. That may be why they asked Him to teach them to pray. We would do well to follow their example and study everything He said about prayer. Perhaps then we could put His principles into practice and really pray as we ought.

Prayer is the inner sanctuary of the Christian life. In the closet of private prayer we meet the Lord. There we can form a close, personal relationship with Him. As a result we can enjoy a growing consciousness of the Holy Spirit's daily guidance, a sweet fellowship with the indwelling Christ, and a quiet confidence in the protection and provision of the Father. There is no peace that passes understanding, no joy unspeakable, no learning to be content in whatever state, except that which is experienced by those who have cultivated a profound personal relationship with God through prayer. We can do that by learning to pray from Jesus' instructions, and having done that, we will have gone a long way toward becoming the people He wants us to be. Let us, therefore, enter into this study with this prayer in our hearts, "Lord, guide us as we examine your word, impress its truths upon us, strengthen us for the task, sustain us when we get weary . . . Lord, teach us to pray!"

## Chapter One
# OUR FATHER

William F. Adeney wrote, "The character of our prayer depends on our conception of God." Let me say it again. The character or quality of our prayer depends on our conception of God, our understanding and appreciation of His nature. Jesus knew that was true, so he taught us to address God in the way that best suits His character, "Our Father." It was not an entirely new way to address the Lord. Isaiah and others in the Old Testament had appealed to Him as Father, but such a lofty understanding of His nature was rare. Jesus taught that it should be the common form of address for the Christian. He would say to us that we should ordinarily think of God as Father. To be sure, He is still the Creator and Sustainer of the universe. He will be our judge. He will ever be awesome in majesty and power. But most often, we should think of Him as our loving Father.

Let's examine what is contained in the concept of God as Father. The Hebrew and Greek words translated *Father* mean, basically, the originator of our lives, the source from which our lives proceed. Then, by usage, they came to refer to our protector and provider as well. The expression, "Abba, Father" is found three times in the New Testament: First in Mark 14:36. Jesus was in Gethsemane, "the wine press," in agony in prayer. He addressed His Father in this way, "Abba, Father, all things are possible unto thee; take away this cup from me: nevertheless not what I will but what thou wilt." Apparently He was expressing His love for the Father in the strongest possible way, and was pressing His plea on the basis of that love. Second, Romans 8:15. "For ye have not received the spirit of bondage again to fear; but ye have received the spirit of adoption whereby we cry, Abba, Father." Here Paul explains that our attitude toward God is based on our adoption as His dear children. Third, Galatians 4:6. "And because ye are sons, God hath sent forth the Spirit of his Son into your hearts crying, Abba, Father."

The word *Abba* is an emphatic form of the Hebrew or Aramaic *'ab* which means, father. It came to be used as a term of endearment. The emphasis is perhaps roughly equivalent to the ecstatic cry of a child who sees his father after a period of separation, and in his excitement he cries out, "Daddy! Daddy!"

## *EARTHLY FATHERS*

As individuals we develop our understanding of the meaning of Father somewhat from our association with our own earthly fathers. When I think of my father, I think of a man of uncompromising integrity and unbending morality. Yet he was a gentle, loving man. I remember him picking me up and nuzzling me. Sometimes he hadn't shaved for a day or two and his beard was rough, but it felt good to a little boy. He felt like a man. He didn't have the softness or the smell of a woman. I could admire him. I wanted to be just like him.

My father had physical strength. He was an electrician. The lower part of his arms was over developed, and his grip was terrific. But it was his strength of character that impressed me most. When he made up his mind to do something, he could do it no matter how much it might hurt. He could deny himself any present enjoyment in order to provide for his family's future. One summer he worked at two jobs for 13 weeks. He drew two paychecks. The second job paid about 50 percent more than his regular job, but it would not, could not continue after that one three month period. So, every week he put that extra paycheck into a savings account. Not just part of it, all of it, for the entire 13 weeks. As far as I know, he never spent one penny of it. To understand how difficult that was, you need to know that we were very poor. I tell people that we were so poor we couldn't afford a dog. My brother and I had to take turns hiding under the porch to run out and bark at strangers. We really were poor. We lacked many things our friends had. So it took real strength to put that money back for an emergency. He had that kind of strength.

I remember working with my father and the pride of feeling that he would rather have me at his side, rather depend on me than any one else. So, when I think of God as Father, I think of strength and reliability and gentleness and willingness to work hard for the benefit of the family He loves so much.

But my father wasn't perfect. Sometimes he was selfish. He could sit for hours with a book. He could lose himself in the world the book created. We could't share that world. He sometimes seemed unaware of our presence when he was reading. Now, I know God isn't like that. He always has time for us. He never thinks only of Himself.

Because earthly fathers are always imperfect, we need to look at the perfect Son to complete our picture of the One who could be Father to such a Son. We must see the perfect loyalty, compassion, devotion, zeal, wisdom, humility, meekness, faith and love of Jesus, and realize that it had its origin in the father.

## *THE PRODIGAL SON*

Christ Himself gave us a beautiful picture of God as Father in the parable of the prodigal son, Luke 15:11-32. He showed us a father who gives his children the freedom to make their own choices. He wants them to accept His way because of His example and because they love Him. He wants them to understand that His love and His wisdom should assure them His way is best. The younger brother in the parable came to that position after his foolish actions had brought him to the brink of despair. But the older brother never understood that. He remained in his father's house not because of his love and appreciation of his father or his father's law, but because he feared the consequences of leaving. It is apparent that he never partook of his Father's spirit. His lack of love for his brother and his focus on himself make that quite clear.

Jesus also showed us a Father who pours out His love on His children without interruption. Our sinful actions do not alter or diminish that love. It is only waiting for our response to express itself. The Father in the parable did not start loving His son again when He saw him coming back home. The love had been there all the time. It only needed the coming of the son to give it the opportunity to express itself. The Father's love was being expressed to the older son every day, but the young man did not recognize it. He never gloried in it, and so did not experience the joy he could have known.

He showed us a Father who is merciful and generous. The younger son was starving in a foreign land. He would have eaten hog food if anyone had given him some. Then he began to think about his Father. He knew Him to be kind, generous, tender hearted and merciful. Then he thought of his own shameful actions and knew his Father must have been hurt by them. Sorrow for sin (II Cor. 7:10) and the goodness of the Father (Rom. 2:4) led him to repent. He made up his mind to go back, to throw himself on the mercy of the Father, not as a son but as a servant. He knew he did not deserve the loving generosity of the Father, but he also knew the character of his Father and he was content to place himself as a servant in His hands. Ah, but the Father's love far outshone the expectations of the son. He was received back not only as a son, but as a beloved and honored son. All was forgiven and forgotten.

## *CHILDREN OF THE FATHER*

When we speak of the Fatherhood of God, the other side of the coin is the fact that we are His children. In one sense all men are. He made us all. He gave us life. He made us in His image, and thus, we are all His children. However, some men have rejected Him as Father, either through an act of rejection or through a passive slide away from Him. They are spoken of in the Bible as "children of wrath" (Eph.2:3) or as being of their "father, the devil" (John 8:44). Through disobedience and rebellion they have aligned themselves with Satan. In actual fact we have all been children of wrath, but some have been reborn into the family of God. They now have a special right to address Him as Father.

We would do well to look again at the process of rebirth as it is outlined in the Bible. First, there is the hearing of the word. It corresponds to the planting of the seed. I Peter 1:23 says we are "born again, not of corruptible seed but of incorruptible, by the word of God . . ." cf. James 1:18, Romans 10:17. Second, there is the accepting of the gospel message as truth, i.e., believing it. This gives one the right to become a child of God (John 1:12). Third, one gains confidence in Jesus Christ, seeing Him as "the way, the truth, and the life." We come to trust Him to the point of turning over our lives to Him, crucifying self (Gal. 2:20; Rom. 6:6) that we might rise up from the watery grave to walk in newness of life, reckoning our old selves dead indeed unto sin and our new selves alive unto God through Jesus Christ our Lord (Rom. 6:11). That is the process of rebirth as it is found in the New Testament. One hears the gospel message which is the power of God for his salvation. He believes it and as its influence grows in his heart, it produces repentance. Then repentance leads to obedience in Christian baptism. He comes out of the water a new creature. He has been born again. If any of you who are reading this have not been born again, you need to do something about it now. It is up to you. If you believe in Jesus, and if you would be willing to turn your life over to Him, you can demonstrate your surrender to Him by being baptized. If you want to be a child of God, you can.

Those who are His children by adoption and rebirth are given awesome responsibilities. We must be "imitators of God as dear children" (Eph. 5:1). That means we must love as He loves, with uninterrupted, unconditional love, love for enemies, as well as friends, love that expresses itself in acts of kindness. Only then, Jesus says, will we be "the children of our Father which is in heaven" (Matt.4:43-47). We must eagerly seek the salvation of sinners and be ready to embrace them wholeheartedly the moment they repent and turn to Jesus. We must be willing to elevate them to the position of beloved brothers (Luke 15:22-24). We who are fathers on earth must seek to be worthy of that title because our little ones will derive their concept of the Heavenly Father through what they see in us.

## *PRAYING TO OUR FATHER*

How, then, should we pray realizing that God is our Father? First, we should meditate upon that relationship. John says, "Behold what manner of love the Father has bestowed on us, that we should be called the children of God!" (I John 3:1). What does it mean to you to have been given the unspeakable privilege of membership in God's family? Does it not give you an overwhelming sense of His goodness? We know He didn't adopt us because we deserved His love. We are sinners, utterly unworthy of the least of His blessings. We are His children, not because we are good, but because He is good. The more we meditate upon that Father-child relationship, the more likely it is that we will bow down our hearts before Him to praise and glorify His holy name. In fact, such meditation will bring us numerous benefits. The deeper our realization of His goodness, the more we will trust Him. The more we trust Him, the more we will be willing to obey His instructions. I could go on and on. We need to focus our thoughts on Him, to contemplate our status as His children. Alexander Maclaren says, "There is inseparable from all prayer the effort to conceive worthily of Him to whom we speak; to raise our souls to that height. This absorbed contemplation is the necessary preliminary of all real prayer, and there is truth in the thought that such losing of self in gazing on God is the highest form of prayer. We should feel as some peasant come to court who stands on the threshold of the presence chamber, and forgetting his grievances and his embassy, gazes entranced on the splendor and benignity of his sovereign." We must never forget that the Father to whom we come is the almighty ruler of the universe, awesome in majesty and power. Yet He is our Father, loving, gentle, and full of tender mercy; our own dear Father. When we think like that, then we will cry, "Oh, Father! My Father!" And, as McClaren also says, "The noblest prayer is Abba, Father."

We must not only meditate on that Father-child relationship, we must petition Him as we would a father. Consider the prayer of Jesus in Mark 14:36. "Abba, Father all things are possible unto thee; take away this cup from me; nevertheless, not as I will but what thou wilt." Notice these things about the prayer of Jesus. First, He expressed His love for the Father in the strongest term available to Him, "Abba, Father." Then He spoke of His confidence in the Father, "All things are possible unto thee." Next came His petition, "Take away this cup from me." Finally, He expressed His total surrender to the Father's will, "Nevertheless, not what I will, but what thou wilt." We should follow that example. That is how we should present our petitions to God. "Oh Father, my Father! You can do anything.Take away this illness from my loved one. Nevertheless, I want what You want. Your will be done." If we pray like that from the heart, we can be sure He is listening.

## *THE PERSONAL PRONOUN*

Now, let me deal briefly with the pronoun, "Our" as in "Our Father." This word reminds us that we are a part of a great family. God has many other children who have as much claim on His love and blessings as we do. Selfishness has no part in the character of the Lord. As His children we must ever seek His strength to eradicate it from our own make up. We must seek blessings for our brothers and sisters in Christ as diligently as we seek them for ourselves.

It is told that the commander of a Roman army had given orders that no one was to approach his tent to disturb him at night. To do so would be to forfeit ones life. One night a soldier did dare to approach his tent. He was seized by the guards who were preparing to carry out the execution when they heard the voice of the commander calling out to them. His instructions were to find out why the young soldier had dared come. He had made up his mind that if he came in his own behalf, the execution would be carried out, but if he came to plead for others, he would be spared. It turned out he had come in behalf of two friends, and the commander was pleased to spare him. Just so, we should never present ourselves before the throne of God for ourselves alone. Remember that the fullest enjoyment of blessings depends on our being willing to share them. To keep all for ourselves is to lose the blessedness of His gifts.

Secondly, this word "Our" reminds us that a personal appropriation of God is necessary for prayer that is real. It is not enough that He is *a* Father. We must know Him as *Our* Father. Here is the grandest object of prayer; to know Him, to be able to cry from a heart overflowing with love, "My Father! My Father!" How blessed eternity will be to those who have cultivated a relationship like that with God.

In the opening words of the model prayer Jesus has shown us God as Our Father, the source of our lives, the protector and provider, the One who loves us unconditionally and uninterruptedly. He has shown us that to pray as we ought we must know Him thus through rebirth and a deep commitment to the cultivation of that Father-child relationship. Let me urge you to make that kind of commitment. I can promise you that you will be greatly blessed and that you'll find your prayer closet has indeed become the inner sanctuary of your Christian life. You will also be able to gain far more from this study if you'll make that commitment here at the beginning.

## Discussion Questions

1. What can we learn from our observance of the way God functions as our Father that will help us be better parents?

2. The way our children behave reflects on us as parents. What does that imply for us as children of God?

3. When you think of God, what words come to your mind? How would you describe Him? Do you think of gentleness, love, mercy, and compassion? Or do you think of majesty, power, dominion, holiness and unapproachable light? Which concept is more nearly correct? Is it possible for us to have all of those ideas as parts of our total concept of God?

4. What kinds of things do you know about God that would lead you to use the term "Abba" or "Daddy" in speaking to Him?

5. How much do thoughts of your Father on earth affect your concept of the Heavenly Father? In what ways do those thoughts mold your concept of God?

6. Have you ever thought of prayer as a means to enter the throne room of God for a private audience with your Creator? How would that concept alter your approach to God in prayer?

7. Have you ever thought of prayer as a means of climbing up into your Daddy's lap to talk to Him about everything? Is that a valid scriptural concept?

## Chapter Two
# FATHER IN HEAVEN

In the four verses which precede the model prayer as it is recorded in Matthew six, Jesus warned us against wrong approaches to prayer. He mentioned the heathen and Pharisaic approaches. The heathens thought their gods would be moved by much speaking, by quantity rather than quality. But, Jesus said that our Heavenly Father already knows our needs. He is not ignorant so that we need to inform Him, nor is he reluctant to bless us so that we need to persuade Him. Our need is simply to lay bare our hearts before Him, to hide nothing from Him of our desires, our motivations, our aspirations, to be totally honest with Him. We are to make Him our most intimate confidant.

The Pharisees weren't thinking about God at all in their

prayers. In Luke 18:10-11 Jesus showed us that the Pharisees' prayers were so completely self-centered it could be said they prayed "with themselves." These are His words, "Two men went up into the temple to pray; the one a Pharisee, the other a publican. The Pharisee stood and prayed thus with himself, God, I thank thee, that I am not like other men . . . ."

In Matthew 6, Jesus says that those hypocrites loved to pray in the synagogues and on street corners that they might be seen of men. They loved to be on their way to the temple when the hour of prayer arrived so they could stop in full view of the public to utter their pious prayers. They wanted to be known as great men of God, great men of prayer. But Jesus says that prayer is to be a thing between you and God alone. The purpose of entering the closet is two-fold. We shut the door to shut out the world and to shut ourselves in with God. We shut out all distractions (the same reason we close our eyes) so we can focus our minds and hearts on the Father. Our prayers should be in secret in the sense that we want to be separated from all men, we should not be concerned about the reaction of any man to our prayers. We should want to be so focused on Him that we are oblivious to anything or anybody else.

So, the gist of Matthew 6:5-8 is this: First, in order to approach God correctly we must forget about men and their opinions of us. It is perfectly legitimate, a worthy, even noble ambition to desire to be a man of prayer. But if it is not legitimate, it is unworthy and ignoble to desire to gain the reputation of a good pray-er. We must pray in secret, shut off from the world and shut in with God, so totally focused on Him that we forget even ourselves as we approach God to worship Him in prayer. Second, we should get rid of the foolish, heathen notion that we can manipulate God by praying long enough or hard enough, that if only we can find the correct formula our prayers will be effectual, we'll get God in a corner and He will be forced to bless us.

Sometimes on the night before the beginning of some great project, an evangelistic crusade or a faith promise rally, we will have an all night prayer vigil. We seem almost to think God is sitting by the clock ready to punch our card when it strikes 7:00 a.m. whereupon He will say, "Congratulations! Your prayer vigil is now completed and you have qualified to have three wishes granted. How do these sound? 1. Overflow crowds at your revival. 2. One hundred baptisms. 3. A two-page documentation of your accomplishments in the periodical of your choice." Perhaps that sounds harsh, but isn't it true that those prayer vigils are often designed to extract blessings from God which will enhance the reputation of the one who organizes them?

Let me hasten to add that it is all right to have an all night prayer vigil if it is done in secret or without calling attention to yourself and if your purpose is to humble yourself and seek God's face and turn from your wicked ways. It is all right to have an all night prayer vigil if some burden is so heavy on your heart that you simply must lay it bare before God in an extended session of prayer. It is all right to have an all night prayer vigil if your purpose is to remind people of their utter dependence on God, and not to attempt to twist His arm through extended prayer so that He is forced to bless you. To hold an all night prayer vigil as a means of coercing God is a heathen rather than a Christian idea. Jesus says that heathens "think that they shall be heard for their much speaking." So, the right way to approach God according to Matthew 6: 5-8 is in secret, shut off from the world, shut in with God, completely focused on Him, in earnest, totally honest, open, and laid bare before Him.

## *ADDRESSING GOD*

Having shown us what was wrong with the heathen and Pharisaic approaches to God in Matthew 6:5-8, Jesus proceeded with the model prayer in verses 9-13. The way He taught us to addess the Lord contains two elements, two phrases which contain converse ideas. "Our Father" expresses an intimate, Father-child relationship. "Which art in heaven" reminds us that our

Father is also the infinite God who created the universe. As His children we are given the unspeakable privilege of being on intimate terms with the infinite God.

Remember, this prayer is a skeleton. It contains all the essential elements of prayer. Martin Luther said there is "nothing more wonderful in the Bible." We study it in order to learn how to pray, to put flesh on the skeleton, that is, to fill out the outline. It is one of the most difficult, yet one of the most rewarding things we do as Christians.

Let's look now at that phrase, "Which art in heaven." The word *heaven* is derived from the old Anglo-Saxon word *heave-on*, meaning to be lifted up or up lifted. So, it implies a place or a state which is high above our commonplace condition on earth (W. Phillip Keller, *A Layman Looks at the Lord's Prayer*, p. 26). The fact that it is a place high above us is confirmed by scriptural usage. Genesis one speaks of fowl flying in the open firmament of heaven and of the stars being placed in the heaven. Job 22:12 asks, "Is God not in the height of heaven?" and says, "Behold the height of the stars, how high they are!" So, it is a place high above us.

That God's dwelling place is also a state high above, far superior to ours is apparent from Isaiah 55:8-9. "For my thoughts are not your thoughts, neither are your ways my ways, saith the Lord. For as the heavens are higher than the earth, so are my ways higher than your ways, and my thoughts than your thoughts." "Nevertheless we, according to His promise, look for new heavens and a new earth, wherein dwelleth righteousness" (II Pet. 3:13). The place where God dwells is a place where there is no sin, no selfishness, no evil. It is a place of unending love. Morally and ethically it is high above the place where we live.

## *THE INFINITE GOD*

What does the word infinite bring to mind? I think, "The

heavens declare the glory of God . . . ." The vastness of the universe is incomprehensible to the human mind. We speak of the distances to the stars in terms of light years, but we can't imagine such distances. We can imagine in miles because our eyes can see that far. From the top of a great mountain we may be able to see hundreds of miles. With a small telescope we can see features of the moon quite clearly, but if I could get into my car and drive to the moon, it would take me nearly two years to get there (driving 500 miles a day, 5 days a week). Yet scientists tell us there are stars they know about which are billions of light years away from earth. The human mind can't comprehend that, but God's mind can. He not only understands the universe, He designed it and made it. He simply spoke it into existence, made out of nothing. The mind and power of God are infinite.

Let me give you another illustration. Consider the rose. Think of the delicacy of its petals, the exquisite beauty of its form, the perfection of its fragrance. The same One who designed the infinite vastness of the universe planned the delicate perfection of the rose. The illustrations are endless: The grandeur of the mountains and of great thunderheads. The amazing capacity of the human mind: analysis, emotion, creativity, invention, courage, humor, suspense, deceit. The wonders of the human body: the eye perceives color, depth instantaneously; the brain records hundreds of facts in seconds; the blood nourishes, supplies with oxygen; DNA, so small, multiplied hundred of times it still can't be seen by the human eye, yet it contains all the information and the capability to direct the cells to produce every physical characteristic a man will ever possess. All these were designed and created by the one who made the vast universe. I say again, the mind and power of God are infinite.

He is infinite in majesty. He dwells in unapproachable light. The vast distances of space are as nothing to Him. Time and speed have no significance to the One who inhabits eternity. The intricacies of the rose and of the human mind and body are child's play to Him who designed and created them. Our proper response to this God of infinite power, wisdom and majesty is to stand in awe before Him, to prostrate ourselves in utter submission to Him, to be overwhelmed, speechless in His presence, struck dumb by His unspeakable greatness.

He is infinite in holiness and purity. When I think of pure motives, I think of the selfless devotion of Anne Sullivan who gave more than 50 years of her life to her pupil, Helen Keller. But Anne Sullivan was human, and even she had moments of less than pure motivation. Somehow I think there may have been just a hint of jealousy in the remark she made on the night she received an honorary doctorate from Temple University. When the ceremony was over, the reporters clustered around Helen. Only one interviewed Anne Sullivan. "Even at my coronation," she remarked, "Helen is queen."

I don't know if Anne Sullivan in an unguarded moment felt a pang of jealousy regarding the fame of Helen Keller. I do know she was human and it is understandable if she felt that way. But our Father in heaven is not like that. His motivation is always perfectly pure, always selfless. It is His very nature. One who loves perfectly does not think of self, but of the loved one. That describes God, for God *is* love.

How should we respond to a God of perfect purity and holiness? Search the scriptures. Examine all the times when people in the Bible had visions of God. You will find that invariably their initial reaction was one of fear. The fear was brought on by their instant recognition of the contrast between their own sinfulness and the holiness of God. Our approach to this holy God, then, ought to be with deepest reverence, godly fear. We should say with Job, "Behold, I am vile; what shall I answer thee? I will lay mine hand upon my mouth" (Job 40:4).

He is infinite in knowledge. We can hide nothing from Him. We cannot deceive Him. We must, therefore, be totally honest with Him; we must bare our hearts before Him.

He is infinite in love, compassion and mercy. He commended His love for us in that while we were yet sinners Christ died for us.

It is conceivable that some of us might be willing to give our lives for someone else. But I cannot imagine loving anyone enough to allow one of my daughters to be tortured and crucified for him — even for the whole world. But God allowed men to do that to Jesus for us, because His love is infinite. We ought to commit ourselves without reservation to the One who loves us that much. Our approach to Him should be as devoted slaves.

Let's reiterate: his mind and power are infinite, so we should stand before Him in awe, speechless, overwhelmed by His infinite majesty. We should prostrate ourselves before Him. He is infinite in purity and holiness, so we should come before Him in godly fear. We should lay our hands upon our mouths and confess our unworthiness. He is infinite in knowledge. We should consciously bare our hearts before Him. He is infinite in love, mercy and compassion, so we should lay down our lives before Him in total surrender as His devoted slaves. Finally, we should remember Jesus taught us that God is our Father, so we should come before Him with deepest gratitude, exclaiming with John the apostle, "Behold, what manner of love the Father hath bestowed upon us, that we should be called the sons of God" (I John 3:1). The infinite God has chosen to adopt us as His own beloved children. In our approach to Him we must keep this whole concept in mind to come to Him as we ought.

## *MAN'S GREATNESS*

Men are never greater than when they pray as Jesus taught us to pray. Great men and women of God have always been people of prayer. Jesus, Himself prayed all night on occasion. Sometimes He got up a great while before daylight to go out into the mountains to pray. Paul made so many references to his prayers, it is evident that he had to spend much time in prayer. Martin Luther and John Wesley spoke of lengthy prayer sessions. Wesley expected that those who truly sought to be God's men and women would spend at least two hours in prayer daily. I know of a time when Mr. and Mrs. Vernon Newland (who founded St. Louis, Dallas, Memphis, Midwest, and Iowa Christian Colleges) spent a whole night in prayer in behalf of a student. It was not that these people kept track of the time so they could congratulate themselves on their prayer lives, but rather, they knew they were in the presence of God. They entered into eternity, as it were. Prayer was life to them; they could not live without it. But, there is nothing more difficult for the Christian than to establish and maintain a consistent, meaningful prayer life. Anyone who has tried it knows what I mean. You find yourself getting stale, going through the motions. It seems meaningless. But Paul said, "Don't stop, keep on praying." The King James Version says, "Pray without ceasing." I think Paul meant that we should not stop, no matter how discouraged we become. Jesus spoke of faithfulness in prayer as a demonstration of real faith (Luke 18:1-8).

I want to challenge you to make a commitment today! Commit yourself to pray, really pray, in your closet. Shut out the world and shut yourself in with God. Be totally honest, lay bare your heart before Him with deepest reverence for the infinite God and warmest love for your heavenly Father.

## Discussion Questions

1. What best illustrates for you the concept of infinite?
2. What are some of the ways in which God is infinite?
3. Why do we go to a private place to pray?
4. Is it necessary to close your eyes to pray? Why do we?
5. Where is heaven? Why does the Bible speak of it as being above us?
6. If God knows our needs so that we don't have to inform Him and if He always desires the best for us so that we don't have to persuade Him, why do we need to pray at all?
7. How does a discussion of an intimate relationship with our infinite God affect you? Does it make you want to cultivate such a relationship?

## Chapter Three
# HALLOWED BE THY NAME

There are several different kinds of prayers. There is the ejaculatory prayer. It is the sudden outcry of a soul in crisis. It may amount to only a word or two or three: "Help!" or "Save me, Father!"or "Please, Lord!" Often the urgency of the crisis precludes a more formal approach to prayer. It might be compared to the plea of a child who, when facing a snarling dog, suddenly spots his father running to the rescue and cries out with tears of relief streaming down his cheeks, "Daddy! Save me!"

There are congregational prayers, those public prayers in which one person prays audibly while the others silently or not so silently say "Amen" to the petitions he offers. There are the shared prayers of those who pray together, having confessed their faults to one another (James 5:16). We don't do enough of that for our own good. There are family prayers when we meet with those who share our homes for a time of family closeness and a corporate approach to the throne of grace. We don't do nearly enough of that either. Of course, there are other types. This list is by no means exhaustive.

The model prayer that Jesus gave us is a model for personal prayers, private prayer, closet prayers, those prayers in which our first purpose is to develop an intimate relationship with our Father in heaven. We must never forget that we are seeking God in our private, closet prayers. Our primary purpose is not to find some secret formula which will make our prayers "effectual." We are not looking for "power in prayer" or the ability to move mountains. We aren't looking for anything God can give us. We are seeking God, Himself! We want an intimate relationship with our Father, the infinite God. That is the greatest blessing of all. It is, of course, perfectly appropriate to include praise, thanksgiving, petition, confession, and intercession in our private prayers, but we must remember, it is God we seek. We want to know the joy of His presence and the peace that comes to those who have learned to sit at their Father's feet and gaze into His face, knowing they have found the best there is in life.

## *POSTURE IN PRAYER*

Let me mention one other thing before we get into the study of the third phrase of the model prayer. You will notice that Jesus gave no instructions concerning an appropriate posture for prayer. There are, however, several places in the Bible where posture in prayer is mentioned. Jesus knelt and lay prostrate on the ground in Gethsemane (Luke 23:41; Matt. 26:39). Elijah went to the ground and placed his face between his knees when he prayed for rain while on top of Mt. Carmel (I Kings 18:42, James 5:17,18). When Hezekiah was told by God's prophet that he was about to die, he "turned his face to the wall" (II Kings 20:2). The Pharisee stood in the temple (Luke 18:10). The publican stood also, but with his eyes turned downward (Luke 18:13). Jesus, thus, implied that the Pharisee looked up as he prayed. The evident implication is that posture is unimportant except as it demonstrates one's attitude. Kneeling may or may not show that a man is humble before God. It may simply be a habit or a form that demonstrates nothing about the condition of a man's heart.

In practice I have found that there is one other factor to be considered regarding one's posture in prayer. It is sometimes difficult for me to stay awake during private prayers. Standing or kneeling, or using Elijah's "face between the knees" posture makes it less likely that I will fall asleep. The following poem makes a final important point about posture in prayer.

**The Prayer of Cyrus Brown**

"The only way for a man to pray," said preacher Dr. Wise,
"Is standing straight with outstretched arms and rapt and upturned eyes."
"Oh, no, no, no," said Elder Snow, "Such posture is too proud.
The only way for a man to pray is with head contritely bowed."
"It seems to me his hands should be austerely clasped in front,
With both thumbs pointing to the ground," said Preacher Dr. Blunt.
"The only way for a man to pray," said Deacon Lemuel Keys,
"And the only proper attitude is down upon his knees."
"Las' year I fell in Hodkins' well," said Farmer Cyrus Brown,
"With both my feet a stickin up and my head a pintin down;
I said a prayer right then and there, bes' prayer I ever said.
The prayinest prayer I ever prayed, a standin on my head."

## *ATTITUDES IN PRAYER*

In the previous two chapters we discussed the address of the Lord's Prayer. We noted that Jesus taught us to approach God as a beloved child approaches his father, and that He immediately moved from that to an expression which reminds us that our God is infinite. So, our attitudes as we come before God should include the intimate feelings of a trusting child for a loving father and the awe-struck reverence of a finite being standing in the presence of the infinite God. Balance is needed, warmest love and deepest reverence, if we are to please God as we come to Him in prayer.

The example of Abraham in Genesis 18:22-33 demonstrates perfectly the attitude God desires in us. Notice how the patriarch combined reverence and boldness. Verse 27 shows his reverence, "Behold now, I have taken upon me to speak unto the Lord, which am but dust and ashes." Verse 25 shows his boldness,"That be far from thee to do after this manner, to slay the righteous with the wicked . . . . Shall not the Judge of all the earth do right?"

## *THE FIRST PETITION*

In this chapter we will study the first of the petitions in this prayer the Lord taught us to pray. We will note the significance of the order of the petitions and the specific meaning and application of this request, "Hallowed be thy name." First of all, then, note the order of the petitions. The first three have to do with bringing glory and honor to God. "Hallowed be thy name, thy kingdom come, thy will be done in earth as it is in heaven." The word "thy" is found in each of them. Thus the emphasis is placed properly. The emphasis is upon God and His glory. That first. Then and only then, the emphasis shifts to us and our needs. "Give us this day our daily bread, and forgive us our debts as we forgive our debtors, and lead us not into temptation, but deliver us from evil." All four petitions have the word "us." All four deal with our needs, but first of all, first in order of preference, first in order of importance is the glory of God. That is the way it should be. That is placing the emphasis where it belongs. But our emphasis is often different from that. Our focus is often all wrong. We are consumed with self-interest. We come to Him complaining about our problems, begging to be relieved of infirmities, asking for success in every venture, impatient if answers aren't to our liking and immediately supplied. Do we think of God as some kind of depository of blessings? Do we really think He must supply them to us upon demand? We ought to be satisfied just knowing we have him as our Father. We ought to be content with whatever He deems appropriate to give us. We ought to be rejoicing because He has forgiven us and adopted us as His children, and our greatest desire should be to honor and glorify His holy name!

Have you, as a parent, ever had the experience of doing something special for your child only to have him or her ask immediately for something more? It is a rather disturbing experience and your initial reaction is likely to be one of disgust. You wonder how they can be so ungrateful. Why does it always take one more things to make them happy, and why don't they ever say, "Daddy, this was perfect. I can't think of anything that would have made it better"?

Of course, if you think about it a little longer, you will probably realize that they are simply human. We are all like that to some degree.

One of the ugliest words in the Greek language is *pleonexia*, the root meaning of which is "a desire for more." In our (KJV) New Testament it is translated *covetous*, and it is included in lists of the most horrible sins; placed alongside such things as extortion, theft, fornication, idolatry, drunkenness, uncleanness, wickedness, deceit, sexual perversion, murder, blasphemy, and hatred of God (See Mark 7:22; Rom. 1:29; I Cor. 5:10,11; 6:10; Eph. 5:3). In Ephesians 5:5 we are told that the one who commits this sin is an idolator. He worships things. He thinks the more he can acquire, the happier he will be. He thinks life consists of the abundance of the things he possesses, and that is exactly what Satan wants him to think. If he worships things, he can't be devoted to Jesus. You can't serve two masters.

To disparage such thinking seems almost un-American, a discrediting of the American dream. Doesn't every American want to "better himself"? Our whole system tends to make us want to keep up with the Joneses. After all the average American family watches more than six hours of television every day. That means we see about a whole hour of commercials each day, all of which are designed to make us want something we don't have. The entertainment shows are often about the super rich or super talented or super macho people. They tend to make us want to be like them.

When you pick up the newspaper, you read about sweepstakes winners, a royal engagement, or the latest millionaire athlete. The ads remind you of some catchy commercial tune, and you go on your way singing the praises of some product you may not even like. It's no wonder we get caught in the trap of always wanting more.

Just now I'm thinking of an application of this idea that doesn't necessarily include the desire for things. The spiritual individual may not be very interested in material things, but he may still get caught up in the pattern of always wanting more. I'm afraid some of us just keep on asking God for one more blessing. Our health may be good, but it could be better. We may have many who love us, but there could be more. I think our Heavenly Father must get thoroughly exasperated with us and wonder why we can't ever be happy with what He has already done for us. After all, He does know what we need, and He is anxious for us to have everything that is good for us.

I have decided I'm going to be very careful about asking for so many blessings and start spending more of my prayer time just thanking Him for being so good to me each day. Of course, I still intend to ask for blessings for others who are in need, and I'll still be seeking strength to help me grow to be more loving, generous, kind, forgiving, and forgetful of myself, in short, more like Jesus. But, then, those prayers are the ones He delights to hear and answer. That would be like having your child say, "Daddy, I don't want any more toys or clothes or money or anything like that, I just want you to show me how to be the kind of person I ought to be. That's all I really want, just to please you." Wouldn't you like to hear that? You can be sure God would too!

When asked, "Which is the great commandment?" Jesus answered, "Thou shalt love the Lord thy God with all thy heart, and with all thy soul, and with all thy mind. This is the first and great commandment. And the second is like unto it, thou shalt love thy neighbor as thyself" (Matt. 22:36-39). Love is, therefore, the very essence of Christianity, and the most striking characteristic of love is its ability to make us forget ourselves, to lay aside all self-interest in our all consuming interest in our beloved. This prayer shows that kind of self-forgetfulness. The one who truly prays like this is concerned first of all for the honor and glory of his Lord.

## *THE MEANING OF "HALLOWED BE THY NAME"*

The word "hallowed" may be the most misunderstood word in the English language. The sound of it is unfamiliar to millions who glibly repeat the The Lord's Prayer. They have said everything from "Harold be thy name" to "Hollywood be thy name," and they haven't taken the time to find out what the word means. Actually, the meaning of "hallowed" is "to make holy; or to show as holy; or to regard as holy." We will look at its meaning within the phrase a little later.

"Thy name" means more than we ordinarily mean by that term. It is not just a casual means of identifying our God. The name of God in the Bible is intended to convey something of His nature, His attributes, and His character, especially as He has revealed them to men. In the Old Testament He revealed truths about Himself under various names: *El* or *Elohim* means "the strong One" and was used particularly when He intended to convey to His people something of His power and dominion. "The eternally self-existent One" is the meaning of the name in Hebrew that we may represent by the four letters YHWH. It is the name the King James translators brought into English as "Jehovah." Most often it is represented in our English Bibles by the words, "The LORD." It is used customarily when the context speaks of the covenant faithfulness and tender mercies of our God.

So, basically, the petition, "Hallowed be thy name," means: "May Your great name (as it is synonymous with Your personhood) be honored, considered sacred, inviolable by all men everywhere. May they feel that to besmirch or sully that name would be a most heinous crime. May You so act as to convince men of Your perfect holiness; and may we, as Your children, be given the ability to convince men of Your holiness by the lives we live." By placing this petition first in His model prayer, Jesus has shown us that our first concern, our highest priority as Christians ought to be that all men everywhere would honor and reverence the name of our Father, God.

## *MEN MUST HEAR THE GOSPEL*

Before men can honor the name of our God, they must know about Him. Hundreds of millions of souls in India, China, and most of Asia have never even heard the name of Jesus, but we have the capability to do something about that. In fact, there has never been a generation which had the tools we have to enable us to complete the task of taking the gospel to the whole world.

Three tools have been placed in our hands which make the goal of worldwide evangelism attainable in our times. Communications is the first key. Electronic communications, radio, television, and satellites, make even the most remote corners of the world accessible to the gospel message. Several years ago I saw some slides which were shown by a missionary who had returned from Southeast Asia. One of them showed a primitive village. A native of that village was seated next to a grass hut with a transistor radio in his hand. Even very remote areas can be reached by radio broadcasts of the gospel. Modern printing techniques enable us to print the message in the language of the people to whom it is being sent. Modern linguistic science has enabled translators in our times to reduce hundreds of spoken languages to a written form, and to translate portions of the Bible into those languages. It is conceivable that every known language could have a Bible portion within one generation. We can get the message to them.

Transportation is the second tool. Airplanes, helicopters, landrovers, and motor boats have brought remote areas within a few hours of gospel outposts all over the world. We can take the message to the lost.

Finance is the third tool. The church is big enough. It has enough people. We could give enough to finance mission enterprises in every area of the world. We lack only the commitment. The Christian churches and Churches of Christ in the United States are capable of giving $50 million per year if we would. The non-instrumental brethren could do as much. One hundred million dollars per year could finance missions which could get the message to all the world in this generation. Do we really desire that all men, everywhere honor the name of our God? It is up to us to use the resources we have to get the job done.

In the second place, men must not only know about God, they must know God if they are to honor Him properly. The so-called Christian West is filled with people who know something about our God. They know of Him, but they don't know Him. Some of them don't want to know Him. They have an obstinate desire to go their own way. They have determined to ignore Him so they can continue to live a depraved life style. Others don't know Him because we haven't shown Him to them. Men have not rejected Christianity. They have rejected the parody of Christianity they have seen in the lives of those who claim to be Christians. When men see Jesus in us, when they see His love, compassion, kindness and generosity, they will want to know Him. When they come to know Him, when they experience in their own lives the blessedness of a personal relationship with the living Lord, when they find the peace that comes from knowing He constantly cares for them, when they discover they have been set free from man's rat race and have been given a song in the heart, then they will honor the blessed name of our God. They will want all men everywhere to know Him and honor Him. They will pray sincerely, "Hallowed be thy name!"

If we do pray that prayer sincerely, it binds upon us the responsibility to so live that men may "see our good works and glorify our Father" in heaven. We may repeat those words and then go out and sully the name we wear by our actions, but if we are sincere in our desire to honor Him, our lives will testify to that fact. Men who go to church and say those words also curse, swear and profane His name in the work place. In so doing, they demonstrate their hypocrisy and make a mockery of religion. Sincere men guard their lips and lives. This poem, written about earthly fathers, could apply as well for the children of God. We wear the name our heavenly Father gave us (Acts 11:26).

You got it from your father
It was all he had to give.
So it's yours to use and cherish,
For as long as you may live.
If you lose the watch he gave you,
It can always be replaced,
But a black mark on your name, Son,
Can never be erased.
It was clean the day you took it,
And a worthy name to bear,
When he got it from his father,
There was no dishonor there.
So make sure you guard it wisely,
After all is said and done
You'll be glad the name is spotless
When you give it to your son.

Much of that does not apply, but the idea is there. Our conduct must honor the Father. It can put black marks on His name in the eyes of men. We must carefully guard our ways to see to it that that does not happen.

## *CONCLUSION*

When we come to God in prayer, our first petition, our foremost desire, should be that the name of our God be held in highest honor among all men. It should be our hope that they all will consider that name sacred, inviolable. If that desire is foremost, it will be evident in the lives we live. His Spirit will truly be in us for to put that plea first, we must forget ourselves.

How do you measure up? Is your Christianity nothing more than a fire escape? Do you go through the motions of church attendance and tithing just to keep out of an eternal hell? Is your heart any different from the heart of your unchristian neighbor? Is there any real love for God and your fellowman in you? Are you really a "new creature" because of His Spirit within you? Is your Christianity the real thing? Do you desire above all that men will come to know Him and honor His blessed name?

## Discussion Questions

1. What is wrong with the desire to have "power in prayer?"
2. What is the greatest purpose of prayer?
3. How important is posture in prayer? What does it signify?
4. Can you give an example of the proper balance of reverence and boldness in prayer? From the Bible. From your own experience.
5. Is there any significance in the order of the petitions Jesus taught us in the Lord's Prayer? Do you think most people have their priorities right in their private prayers? If not, why not?
6. What do the names of God teach us about Him and His personhood?
7. Can you explain the difference in knowing about God and knowing Him? Why is it important to know God?
8. How can we lead people to hallow or to give proper reverence to the name of our God?

## Chapter Four
# THY KINGDOM COME

On September 17, 1787 the Constitution of the United States was accepted and signed by the 39 members of the convention in Philadelphia. They immediately presented it to congress which in turn submitted it to the states for their approval. By the following summer it had been ratified by eleven of the thirteen states. So, on March 4, 1789 a new government was inaugurated, and the constitution became the supreme law of this land. For almost 200 years it has remained in force. Let me remind you of the familiar words with which it begins.

> We, the people of the United States, in order to form a more perfect union, establish justice, insure domestic tranquility, pro-

vide for the common defence, promote the general welfare, and secure the blessings of liberty to ourselves and our posterity, do ordain and establish this Constitution for the United States of America.

I want you to notice the things which the writers thought the Constitution ought to do for the citizens of this country.

1. Form a more perfect union between the states.
2. Establish justice for all.
3. Insure domestic tranquility, which I assume meant a peaceful existence between neighbors which would be possible only if the citizens would abide by the laws. Thus, they justified the establishment of police forces.
4. Provide for the common defense. In this way they justified the establishing of the military.
5. Promote the general welfare. The levying of taxes and the use of those taxes for the building of roads, setting up of fire departments and garbage collection would come under this provision.
6. Secure the blessings of liberty for themselves and their posterity.

Many people believe the Constitution of the United States to be the most nearly perfect document of its kind ever written. Of course, it had to be amended almost immediately to include the "Bill of Rights." The two together have stood the test of time. In almost 200 years further amendments have been added only about once a decade on the average. There have been some horrendous interpretations of the Constitution such as the Roe vs. Wade decision of 1973 which made abortion on demand from conception to birth the law in all 50 states. That decision was based on a "woman's right to the privacy of her own body," a right which an activist court invented. Certainly the Constitution mentions no such right. But, by and large, the Constitution has served the American people extremely well. No other document on earth can claim a comparable record. However, no one would suggest we have a perfect government. The system of checks and balances which the Constitution provided has held down the abuses, but not eliminated them. Some would claim our system comes closer to perfection than any other. Perhaps they are right, but I can tell you of another system which could be better, one which would grant perfect justice and equality to all. The Jews knew about it hundreds of years before the birth of Christ. The original idea may have come from an earlier culture which was centered not many miles north of Israel.

## *THE SHEPHERD KING*

Thirty-four miles southwest of Aleppo in modern day Syria at a place called Tell Mardikh archaeologists have uncovered the ruins of an ancient city. The digging began in 1964, but it was not until 1973 that the most dramatic archaeological discovery of the 20th century was made. In a room of the palace ruins of more than 14,000 clay tablets were uncovered. They tell the story of a city and an empire named Ebla which dominated the Near East 4,300 years ago.

As scholars began to study the tablets, they found some fascinating parallels with the Bible. There were similar names and customs. The greatest king of Ebla was named Ebrum, and he may have been the man the Bible calls Eber. The variation in spelling could easily be the result of translation from one language to another. Eber was an ancestor of Abraham, and some think the word Hebrew was derived from his name, that it means "a descendant of Eber." Certainly the cultural backgrounds of Ebla and Israel are similar.

Now, here is a fact from Ebla which relates directly to our topic: The citizens of that city called Ebrum their shepherd. The idea that an ideal king would care for his people as a good shepherd cares for his sheep may have originated there. Centuries later the Hebrew people carried that ideal in their hearts. Of course, Israel's love for that concept was greatly enhanced by the fact that her greatest king came to the throne after having been a shepherd boy. Later he sang the praises of the perfect shepherd King in the beautiful 23rd Psalm.

Consider what David said there: First, a good shepherd provides the best food and water for his sheep. Second, he protects them from their enemies. Third, he lifts them up when they are cast down, and fourth, he leads them in the way that is best for them. He cares for them so well, in fact, that they declare, "I have no wants . . . I fear no evil . . . My cup runs over . . . Surely goodness and mercy shall follow me all the days of my life . . . And I am content to remain in his care forever."

Hundreds of years after David wrote those words, at a time when the glory of Israel was gone and the kingdom was digressing toward its downfall at the hands of Babylon, Isaiah wrote of a glorious kingdom that would come. It would be a time when God's anointed One, the Messiah, would sit on the throne of David and re-establish the honor and glory of Israel. He said of the Messiah:

> His name shall be called Wonderful, Counselor, the Mighty God, the Everlasting Father, the Prince of Peace. Of the increase of his government and of peace there shall be no end, upon the throne of David, and upon his kingdom, to order it, and to establish it with judgment and with justice from henceforth even forever (Isaiah 9:6-7).

You can see how they would think the Kingdom of the Messiah would be perfect. A perfect king would need to provide for his people perfectly, protect them perfectly, rule with perfect wisdom, care for them with perfect love, administer perfect justice, and bring in perfect prosperity. The King Isaiah described would do all of those things. He would rule with perfect wisdom, for He would be called Wonderful Counselor. He would give perfect protection from their enemies, for He would be the Mighty God. He would care for them with unending love, for He was the

Everlasting Father. He would bring in perfect prosperity, for His government would always be on the increase, and peace would never end. He would administer perfect justice from the throne of David forever. There could not be a better government than that.

But after Isaiah wrote those words about the coming Messiah and His kingdom, the Jews suffered century after century of oppression and abuse from various conquering peoples, from Babylon, Persia, Greece, Egypt, Syria, and Rome. So, when John the Baptist appeared on the scene preaching the electrifying message, "The time is fulfilled, and the kingdom of God is at hand. Repent, and believe the gospel," you can imagine the response. The people were weary of oppression. They longed for the coming of the Messiah. They prayed earnestly and fervently that the kingdom would come.

Then, when Jesus came healing their sick and feeding the multitudes, they thought, "Here is the One who can provide for us and protect us. He can feed us when we get hungry even if there is very little food available. He can heal us if the enemy should wound us. He cares deeply for us when we hurt. Surely He is the promised One. Surely He will soon re-establish David's throne. The Romans will be driven out, and the kingdom of prosperity and peace and justice will be ushered in. Hallelujah!"

But, then we know their ideas of the kingdom were wrong. Jesus didn't come to establish an earthly kingdom. He came to establish a spiritual one. Ah, yes, of course, but think of how fervently they must have prayed, "Thy kingdom come!" They wanted it with their whole hearts.

## *DESIRING THE KINGDOM*

Should we want it less? We know what He meant when He taught us to pray about the kingdom. He meant the church. He was teaching us to pray that the church might be established in every place, that the leaven of Christ might leaven the whole world. He meant that we should desire to see all men give allegiance to Him, that they would crown Him King of their hearts. He was teaching us to pray for the coming of the kingdom of grace, that righteousness and peace and joy in the Holy Spirit might be the norm in the lives of people all over the world. He meant that we should pray for the coming of the kingdom of glory when the kingdoms of this world will become the kingdom of our Lord and of His Christ when He shall reign forever and ever. He was teaching us to pray that the glorious day of His coming when every knee shall bow and every tongue confess that Jesus Christ is Lord to the glory of God the Father might come soon.

We must pray earnestly for His kingdom, the church, that it might be established in all nations, that all people would become its citizens. Satan is doing everything in his power to prevent that from happening, and we need the help of the Lord to carry on with this task. We must pray daily for that help and guidance and strength.

The church, the kingdom of light, is locked in a death struggle with the kingdom of darkness. Make no mistake about it, this is not a friendly skirmish. Satan means to destroy the church, and he will use anything he can get his hands on in this fight.

In the West he uses materialism. If he can just get people to desire more and more things, he can make them devote all their time and energy to the acquisition of those things, and they will have no time for the Lord and His church. He uses humanism with its teaching of evolution. He uses hedonism, the pursuit of pleasure. He uses the occult, Eastern religions, ignorance, fear, pride, animal passions, liquor. The names of his tools are legion. But Satan cannot win the war. There will come a day when the old dragon, the devil, will be cast down to hell. Jesus will be the victor, and His faithful ones will reign with Him.

## *COMMITTED TO THE KINGDOM*

There should be in each of us Christians a fierce competitive spirit, an intense desire to see Satan defeated, righteousness established on earth, precious souls snatched from his grasp. If our desire to defeat the devil is what it ought to be, we will work incessantly, give sacrificially, and pray diligently for his defeat. "Oh," but you say, "I do desire fervently the defeat of Satan. I long to see the day when bars and liquor stores would close down for lack of business, and pornography would disappear from the newsstands because no one would buy it, and the television would have wholesome, family programing, and the churches would be filled with sincere worshippers, and men would stop cheating on their wives, and divorce would be unheard of, and crime would cease, and the jails would be empty, and a man's word would be his bond, and people would care as much for their neighbors as they do for themselves. Oh, how I would love to see a time like that! But, I have a family to provide for, and grass to mow, and the oil should be changed in my car, and the washing machine broke down, and I have to see about getting it fixed, and my son is playing in the football game Friday night, and on and on and on. How could I possibly work incessantly for the defeat of Satan? My daughter needs braces on her teeth, and my car needs new tires, and property tax is coming due, and my son has just started to college. How can I possibly give sacrificially to the cause of defeating Satan?"

"Ah, but praying is something I can do. I can pray diligently for the expansion of the kingdom. I can pray for Satan to be defeated. Every afternoon when I go to pick up my son from football practice, while I sit in the car waiting for him, if no one comes over to talk to me, I'll use that time to pray for the defeat of Satan!"

Do you really think God would honor a prayer like that? Do you think He will give you something for which you are unwilling to work or sacrifice?

How can you change your attitudes? How can you become concerned enough to work and pray and give for the expansion of the kingdom?

You can pray for strength to change your priorities, to recognize how many of the things you do are not really important. We should pray, "Thy kingdom come," in the sense of the kingdom of grace coming into our own hearts and those of all who want to know Jesus.

It is not enough for men to give lip service to the King. They must be devoted to Him truly, for it is only as they devote themselves to Him that they find peace and joy and righteousness in their lives. Righteousness comes first. People must turn from the pollution of the world, give up their beer and pornography and foul language, and devote themselves to serving the Lord and their fellow men. Peace follows righteousness. When a man stops struggling for things and starts laying up treasures in heaven, he begins to find peace. When he stops worrying about what men think of him and starts seeking only to please the Lord, he has set his feet on the road to peace. When he accepts his own inability to save himself and relies totally on the forgiving, saving grace of the Lord, he will find he has real peace.

Joy is the result of right thinking. It comes from exulting in the fact that the Lord Jesus is with him always. It comes from knowing that the love of Jesus will never let him go. It comes from realizing how greatly He has honored us by allowing us to be called his children and trusting us with the task of laboring with Him for the salvation of souls. It comes from recognizing what a privilege it is to serve One who loves us so much. We will never pray that others might experience that peace and joy until we have known it ourselves, and we will never know it until we devote ourselves to Him without reservations.

We pray, "Thy kingdom come," and mean, "May the day of Your coming and the beginning of the heavenly kingdom come soon!" Do you long for His coming? You won't unless you are sure you are ready! Are you?

## Discussion Questions

1. Why did the Jews of Jesus' time long for the coming of the kindgom of the Messiah?

2. How did the 23rd Psalm affect the thinking of the Jews concerning the perfect king?

3. What kind of things should we expect to receive from the Lord as our King?

4. How should we conduct our lives considering the fact that we are citizens in the kingdom of our Lord, children of the King, and ambassadors for our King?

5. How can the church be compared with a kingdom? What services does it provide for its members which are comparable with the services a kingdom provides for its citizens?

6. If we sincerely pray, "Thy kingdom come," what obligations are we indebted to fulfill?

7. What kinds of things does Satan use in his fight to destroy the church? How are we to combat those things in the Spirit of Christ?

8. What is the Kingdom of Grace? What is the Kingdom of Glory? How are they different from the Kingdom, the church? How are they the same?

## Chapter Five
# THY WILL BE DONE

We need to focus on two important purposes in our study of the model prayer. First of all, we want to understand what Jesus would teach us about how we should pray. We want our prayer lives to be more nearly what He would have them to be. Second ly, then, we want to make the proper applications of the principles He taught so our lives will be consistent with our prayers.

We have discovered that the way we pray reveals a great deal about our attitudes. We include in our petitions those things which are important to us, and we leave out the unimportant. We even put things in the order of our priorities without doing so consciously. We also demonstrate what we think about God, Himself, by the way we address Him in prayer.

Jesus began the model prayer by showing us the proper way to address God. We should come before Him as children approaching a loving Father while never forgetting that we are finite, mortal, sinful creatures who enter the presence of an infinite, immortal, holy God. We should love Him as our Father and reverence Him as the One who dwells in heaven, the One who inhabits eternity.

Then He showed us what our priorities ought to be. More than anything else, we should desire to see the name of our God honored by all men. Then we should desire that His throne be established in the hearts of people everywhere, and we should long for His will to be obeyed as eagerly and as completely by men on earth as it is by the inhabitants of heaven. Those are the first three petitions of the Lord's Prayer, and they show us that His honor, His kingdom, and His will should be our primary concerns.

## *GOD'S WILL*

In this chapter we will examine the phrase, "Thy will be done." We will look first at its meaning and then seek to discover what His will is for us as individuals.

The meaning of the phrase is simple enough. The will of God is whatever He plans, purposes or desires. When we pray, "Thy will be done," we are expressing our wish that everything He purposes and desires will come to pass. We want all of creation to yield to His will whether it be men or nations or the natural forces of the universe. Of course, we know that only men and their organizations are slow to respond to His will. So, practically speaking, we are praying that human beings will get in line with the rest of creation and bow to the wishes of God.

Right here is where we need to spend most of our energies in this study. We need to discover what His will is for us as individuals so we can make sure we conform to that will. However, the most we can do in the short space we have is to look at His desires for us in broad, basic terms. It wouldn't be possible to do an exhaustive study of His will even if we had much more time. That is the work of a lifetime. It ought to be the major work to which we commit our lives, i.e., coming to know and to do the will of God in everything. You see, our God has a vital interest in everything we think and do, and only constant study of His word throughout our lives will suffice to make us understand His will in all things.

We will look at His will for all men first. Then we will consider what His will is for all Christians, and lastly we will consider His will for those who are mature in Christ.

His desire for all men is that they be saved (I Tim.2:4). Hell was made for the devil and his angels (Matt. 25:41). God never intended for men to go there. Ephesians 1:3-14 clearly states that He planned for our redemption before He made the world. It was "according to the good pleasure of His will" to adopt us as His children, to make us holy and blameless, and to redeem us by the blood of His own dear Son.

As His children, we inherit all the blessings and responsibilities of heaven's royal family. We are expected to act like children of the King of kings, to walk worthy of that name. Those who do will enjoy their Father's home with Him when this life is over.

His plan provides for our cleansing from every stain of sin. We stand before Him spotless, without blame because of the pardon He arranged for us before we were born. The plan further provided that we be consecrated to His service, set apart, sanctified, and marked by the Holy Spirit whom He sends to dwell in us.

Redemption is also a part of that plan. The price to buy us back from slavery in sin was paid when Jesus gave His life for us. We are redeemed by the blood of the Lamb of God. We sold ourselves into slavery when we sinned, but He bought us back with that awful price.

I Timothy 2:4-6 says that He intended those blessings for all men. Verse four states that it is His will that all be saved, and verse six indicates that He gave His life as a ransom for all. He is not willing that any should perish. He wants all to be redeemed (II Peter 3:9). That puts it squarely in our hands. If you have not been redeemed, it is up to you to do something about it. His will is that you be saved. What is your will?

Let's look at what the Bible says He requires from you to claim the pardon He provides. First, it says you must have faith to please Him. Hebrews 11:6, "Without faith it is impossible to please him, for he that cometh to God must believe that he is and that he is a rewarder of them that diligently seek him." So, you see, you must believe that God exists and that He will give you the reward He has promised if you seek Him. In other words, you must trust in His promises. Secondly, the Bible says you must repent. Acts 17:30 says that God now "commands all men everywhere to repent." That means you must make up your mind to turn away from sin so you can do His will. You must remove yourself from the driver's seat of your life, turn the wheel over to Him, make Him your own personal king, give Him the throne of your life. Then the Bible says you must acknowledge your faith and be baptized. In Matthew 10:32 Jesus said, "Whosoever therefore shall confess me before men, him will I confess also before my Father which is in heaven." Romans 10:10 says, "For with the heart man believeth unto righteousness; and with the mouth confession is made unto salvation." Acts 2:38 tells us that baptism follows repentance and procures forgiveness for us. "Repent, and be baptized every one of you in the name of Jesus Christ for the remission of sins, and ye shall receive the gift of the Holy Ghost."

That is what the Bible says about how you claim the pardon Jesus provided for you. It isn't all the Bible says on the subject, but it is a brief outline you can follow today and lay hold on salvation. If you haven't done it, I urge you to do it today!

## *HOLY LIVING*

Now, let's consider God's will for those who are already

Christians. Another passage of Scripture which speaks of the will of God is I Thessalonians 4:3, "For this is the will of God, even your sanctification." To sanctify means to make holy. The context of this passage makes it quite clear that he is referring to holy living. God wants us to live lives that are holy, undefiled, uncorrupted by the world. The Christian should be easily distinguished from his pagan neighbors by his lifestyle. He is set apart from them not just by the things he doesn't do, but even more by the way he talks and by the things he does.

His speech is sanctified. I don't mean he talks in ecclesiastical terminology. He doesn't necessarily use such phrases as, "Praise the Lord," all the time, but he is careful to guard his tongue. He doesn't lie, nor does he need to emphasize his words with oaths. His "yes" means "yes" and his "no" means "no", and everybody knows it. He doesn't cut people down with his words, but builds them up. He considers it a privilege to speak encouraging, uplifting words. He doesn't engage in gossip. He asks himself, "Is it true? Is it kind? Is it helpful?" before he repeats anything about anyone. He knows that frequent references to sex and/or bodily functions don't add spice to his language. They just make it incredibly vulgar, so he refrains from such usage. He does not use the name of God or Jesus in his speech unless it is to give honor to those holy names. He knows that if he used those names as expletives, it would profane them and would put him in the class of those who are not loyal to their Lord. I could say a great deal more about sanctified speech, but you know how to make your words honor the Lord. It is His will that your speech be sanctified. Can you pray "Thy will be done" in regard to your speech without blushing?

God desires that our thinking be sanctified. Philippians 4:8 tells us the kind of things we are supposed to think about, things that are true, honest, just, pure, lovely, of good report, things that are virtuous and praiseworthy. God has given us the ability to control what we think about. Certainly, there are thoughts that come to us unbidden, but we can quickly banish them by turning our thoughts to something else. We control our thinking by controlling the stimuli, by controlling what we read, what we look at, what we listen to, what we talk about. No one can think about things that are pure, lovely, of good report, virtuous and praiseworthy while he is watching a filthy movie on T.V. or at the theatre. Our minds don't work that way, and you know it. However, there is plenty of good reading material available that will promote good, holy thinking. My wife and I have recently read *The Shepherd of the Hills*. I recommend it to you. It is both entertaining and inspirational. I recommend Grace Livingston Hill's novels for light, entertaining reading. You may not agree with all her theology, but you will be uplifted. I would say the same thing about George MacDonald's novels. He was the favorite author of C.S. Lewis. There are a great many non-fiction books that will bless you greatly. If you want your thinking to conform to the will of God, it must be sanctified, holy. It is up to you to make it that way by controlling the input. (Other books I recommend: The Little House books, *The Chronicles of Narnia, Joni, The Hiding Place, Christi, The Beloved Invader, The Lighthouse, Two From Galilee, Anne of Green Gables* and the rest of Anne series. Most of these books are available at Christian book stores. (Many of them may be in your church library.) There are also many really good videos available for family entertainment and instruction.

God desires that our recreation be sanctified. It certainly can be. There are all kinds of wholesome games you can play as a family or as individuals. (Dungeons and Dragons is not one of them!) You don't have to watch T.V. or go to the movies.

I want to say something to the young people that may not be very popular. I went to my last dance more than 20 years ago. I was dating a girl who was in nurse's training. They were having a dance at the school and she wanted me to take her, so I did. We had not been there long when I said to her, "Let's get out of here." Those young people were making, as a part of their dances, explicitly sexual motions toward each other. They were using the dance as an excuse to perform like uncivilized barbarians acting out their fantasies toward each other. It was disgusting, revolting. I felt, and still do, that a Christian had no business in a place like that. I find it hard to believe that one can honor the Lord on a dance floor. I believe churches would be wise to do something to give their young people an exciting alternative activity on prom night each year. They need to plan some activity their youth can really enjoy instead of the dance. God intends for our recreation to be holy.

## *GIVING THANKS*

Finally, let's look at God's will for the mature Christian. I Thessalonians 5:16-18 says, "Rejoice evermore, Pray without ceasing. In everything give thanks: For this is the will of God in Christ Jesus concerning you."

I don't believe that means we are to be Pollyannas, living happy-go-lucky lives, laughing at adversity, pretending sorrow and heartache don't exist. There will be difficult times for us. We will face many, many sorrows. We will suffer, perhaps even more than worldly people. But in the deepest recesses of our minds, in the place where the very foundations of our thinking and our attitudes are found, there is a calmness, a serenity, a sweet realization that we are children of God and that will always be a reason for rejoicing. We will always have a reason to give thanks.

Further, I believe it means we can always be thankful that the will of God is being carried out in our lives even in the midst of suffering. The apostles rejoiced after having been beaten because they were counted worthy to suffer for the cause of Christ (Acts 5:41). Evidently that means they were glad God considered them mature enough in the faith to allow them to suffer, knowing they would remain faithful, knowing persecution would not turn their hearts from Him. It put them in the company of the prophets who were also persecuted for their faith and loyalty to God.

The apostle Peter had some interesting comments about suffering and the will of God. "If, when ye do well, and suffer for it, ye take it patiently, this is acceptable with God (I Peter 2:20). "But if ye suffer for righteousness' sake, happy are ye: and be not afraid of their terror, neither be troubled; but sanctify the Lord God in your hearts; and be ready always to give an answer to every man that asketh you a reason of the hope that is in you, with meekness and fear; having a good conscience; that, whereas they speak evil of you, as of evildoers, they may be ashamed that falsely accuse your good conversation in Christ. For it is better, if the will of God be so, that ye suffer for well doing, than for evil doing, for Christ also hath once suffered for sins, the just for the unjust, that he might bring us to God" (I Peter 3:14-18).

From those passages it should be evident that it is sometimes God's will for us to suffer. The very least we could say is that He would rather we suffer than deny him. Then, even in the midst of our suffering, we can give thanks.

The greatest illustration of intense suffering and rejoicing is found in the life of Jesus, Himself. No man has ever suffered greater agony than our Lord experienced in those last hours leading up to and including His death on the cross. When He left the upper room where He had eaten His last meal with His disciples, He crossed the Kidron Valley to the foot of the Mount of Olives. There was an olive orchard where He often went to be secluded from the world to pray. It was called the Garden of Gethsemane. Gethsemane means, "the wine press." Evidently a device for squeezing grapes or for extracting the oil from olives was located there. If you visit Jerusalem today you can see some olive trees that may have been there in the time of Christ.

As they came to the garden, Jesus left eight of the disciples at the gate. He took Peter, James and John a little further into the garden with Him. Matthew, describing the incident, says He "began to be sorrowful and very heavy." The word translated as "very heavy" means, ordinarily, "sated" (Matt. 26:37). It was used to refer to gluttons who so stuffed themselves that all food became repulsive. Matthew was saying that Jesus was completely filled up, sated, with suffering. Then Jesus, Himself, said to His three closest friends, "My soul is exceeding sorrowful, even unto death" (Matt. 26:38). He meant that the burden of mental anguish was so heavy He was about to die under the emotional strain. He could barely endure. Jesus was not exaggerating for effect. He was speaking literally. The truth of His statement can be seen in the fact that a little while later, He threw Himself on the ground and prayed, "O my Father, if it be possible, let this cup pass from me: nevertheless, not as I will, but as thou wilt" (Matt. 26:39). His sweat became great drops of blood falling down to the ground, and God sent angels to minister to Him to strengthen Him for the task of facing the cross (Luke 22:43-44). He was not, I think, crying out in fear of the physical torture and death of the cross. Earlier He had said, "Now is my soul troubled; and what shall I say? Father, save me from this hour: but for this cause came I unto this hour. Father, glorify thy name" (John 12:27-28). I believe He was fighting a reluctance to sever Himself from the perfect fellowship He had always enjoyed with the Father. If He took our sins upon Himself, they would cut Him off from God, their perfect fellowship would be destroyed by our sins. But He won the battle with Himself. He drank the bitter cup. It was our guilt which He took upon Himself that caused Him to cry out from the cross, "My God, my God, why hast thou forsaken me?"

The final commentary on that experience for Jesus can be found in Hebrews 12:2 where the writer tells us that He "For the joy that was set before Him endured the cross, despising the shame, and is set down at the right hand of the throne of God." The awful mental anguish of Gethsemane and the horrible agony of the cross were endurable because there was joy for Jesus in providing a way for us to be saved and in faithfully doing the Father's will. Did you get that? He had joy in the midst of His sufferings because He was opening the gates of heaven for us!

You see! There really are reasons for rejoicing in the midst of all our sufferings. Romans 12:2 says we are not to be "conformed to this world, (but) transformed by the renewing of (our) minds, that (we) may prove what is that good, and acceptable, and perfect will of God." The word translated "prove" in this verse means "to put to the test." It was used in reference to the work of an assayer who tests the ore for the purpose of discovering the value of the gold in it. The idea is that we, by bringing our lives into a continuing conformity with the will of God, may test that will and discover that it is always good, always acceptable. In fact, it is perfect. Nothing could be better for us even if suffering is involved. So, we can give thanks in everything because God is in control and His will is being worked out in our lives.

Let me conclude this chapter by reiterating. The will of God for all people is that they may be saved, adopted into His family and given a home in heaven. The will of God for all Christians is that they live holy lives, that they be sanctified, set apart from the world around them by the purity of their lives and their dedication to the Lord. The will of God for us all as we become more mature in the faith is that we come to the point of giving thanks in all things because we realize God will only allow those things to happen to us which will work out for our ultimate good. There is a great deal of difference in being resigned to accepting God's will even though it is difficult, and in rejoicing in that will in the midst of hard times. It is the latter that God wants from us. He wants us to be so thoroughly convinced that what He allows is for our good that we rejoice in His will even when we are hurting. That is mature faith!

## Discussion Questions

1. Why is it not possible to learn the will of God for every particular of our lives in a short time?

2. If God desires that all people be saved, why did He make a hell?

3. When we pray, "Thy will be done," what obligations accrue to us as a result?

4. Do you think most of us really want God's will for our lives? If we do, why don't we rejoice and feel content in whatever state we find ourselves?

5. If we are to give thanks "in everything," does that mean *for* everything? Should a person thank God that he has cancer, for example, or should he just find reasons to thank God in spite of the fact he has the disease?

6. What do we mean by "sanctified speech, thinking, and recreation?" Can you show how one can make his speech and thinking holy? What types of recreation do you consider wholesome?

7. What should a Christian do when he is invited to participate in some activity which he is not sure would honor the Lord?

8. How can we take a stand for righteous living among our friends, co-workers, and/or fellow students without being obnoxious?

## Chapter Six

# IN EARTH AS IT IS IN HEAVEN

The words "in earth as it is in heaven" have no meaning apart from the phrase that precedes them, "Thy will be done." They qualify that phrase by specifying the manner in which God's will is to be done. The wish Jesus was teaching us to express may be fairly represented thus, "May men on earth do thy will as eagerly and as thoroughly as do the inhabitants of heaven."

It is evident in the various visions of heaven described in the Bible that all the heavenly beings obey God instantly and gladly. They are ever presented as singing His praises, falling down before Him to worship, rushing to do His bidding, and serving Him eagerly with adoring hearts. Consider just one such vision, Revelation 4:8-11.

> And the four beasts had each of them six wings about him, and they were full of eyes within: and they rest not day and night, saying Holy, Holy, Holy, Lord God Almighty, which was, and is, and is to come. And when those beasts give glory and honour and thanks to him that sat on the throne, who liveth forever and ever, the four and twenty elders fall down before him that liveth forever and ever, and cast their crowns before the throne, saying, Thou art worthy, O Lord, to receive glory and honour and power: for thou hast created all thing, and for thy pleasure they are and were created.

The four beasts, or rather, "living creatures" as most later translations designate them, are represented as having six wings. No doubt they are the same creatures Isaiah calls seraphim (Isa. 6:23). Those creatures also had six wings and cried "Holy, Holy, Holy!" Isaiah tells us they shielded their faces from the glory of God with one pair of wings, covered their feet with another pair, and used the third pair to fly. Ezekiel described similar creatures in the first chapter of his book and took great pains to explain how they moved very quickly in any direction at the will of God's Spirit. Taken all together, these visions tell us of creatures who respond immediately to the command of God, evidently doing so because they truly adore Him. That is the kind of obedience Jesus taught us to pray would be found on earth, instant, adoring obedience to the will of God.

## *YIELDING TO THE MASTER POTTER*

If we pray "Thy will be done, in earth as it is in heaven" sincerely, we must be eager to do that will ourselves. We must surrender ourselves to Him as clay in the hands of the Potter (Jer. 18:1-6, Rom. 9:20-21). W. Phillip Keller in his book *A Layman Looks at the Lord's Prayer*, describes the work of a primitive potter in beautiful, poetic terms. He makes comparisons I believe the Lord would have us make when considering this analogy. I want to share some of his points with you. He begins by describing the selection of a lump of clay from a stinking, horrible pit,and compares that with God's gentle care as He lifts the sinner up from the foul pit of sin. He mentions the precision with which the potter centers the clay lump on the rotating stone, and compares that with the way our Lord seeks to center our lives in our Rock, Jesus Christ. Mr. Keller then tells of the light he saw in the eyes of the master potter as he envisioned what that clay could become and compares that to God's eager anticipation as He thinks about the lovely vessel He can produce if the sinner/clay will respond to His touch. Then he tells of the disappointment as the potter discovers bits of sand in the clay, hard little bits which cannot be shaped by his touch, and which make it impossible for him to fashion a masterpiece of pottery. Keller makes a comparison between those bits of sand and the resistance the Lord encounters in us, resistance which forces Him to settle for second best in us. If we had yielded all to our Master Potter, He could have made a vessel of surpassing loveliness with our lives. He would have been greatly honored by such a vessel, but because we refuse to do His bidding in some things, He can only make of us a common utensil. The choice is ours. To yield in every way will be painful and difficult, but the final product will be so much more satisfying if we will crucify self and surrender completely to His will.

I want to elaborate a little more on that last thought. Most of us have had opportunities to make some great sacrifice for the Lord. Often we are unwilling to go that far. There may be someone reading these lines who could have given up a secure future in business to become a missionary. Perhaps you wanted to give your life to some primitive tribe to give them the message of Christ, to give them hope in Him, but someone convinced you it was not practical. So, now you are successful in the eyes of the world. You have a nice home, a lovely family, all the things you would think it takes to make someone happy. But something is missing. It could be that when you said "No" to the mission field, God had to settle for second best in your life. You are not an

Albert Sweitzer or a J. Russell Morse or a Cameron Townsend today because you didn't give the Potter complete control of your life.

Cameron Townsend was a Bible salesman in Central America who couldn't even speak the language of the people to whom he was sent. No one thought he would last one summer, but they didn't realize he would feel God calling him to learn that unwritten language and translate the New Testament for those people. Because he was willing to live under incredible hardships, because he said "Yes" to the Master Potter, and because hundreds have followed in his footsteps, today, about 70 years later, portions of the New Testament have been translated into more than 500 languages which formerly had no portion of the Bible. Thousands, perhaps millions of people have heard the message of Jesus Christ because Cameron Townsend did not allow difficult circumstances to alter his commitment to give the Potter complete control of his life.

How about you? Do you want God to make you a vessel of surpassing loveliness? Do you want Him to use you to touch countless lives? If you want that, it may mean tremendous sacrifice. You may have to leave friends and family far behind. You may have to face many hardships. You may have to forfeit what seems like real security so you can trust Him for your security. What kind of vessel do you want God to make of you? Do you want to be all He wants you to be, or do you think second or even third best will be all right?

Please don't misunderstand me. I know that most of us, perhaps all of us, lack the talent and intelligence of an Albert Sweitzer. We couldn't be successful concert organists or renowned authors. But, after all, it wasn't his talent or his intellegence that made his name a household word. It was his heart. It was the size of his compassion. It was his love for an unlovely people, his willingness to endure pain and separation from those he loved most in order to serve a people who needed him that made him memorable. We probably don't have his talent or intelligence, but we could have his compassion if we would allow the Master Potter to mold us into what He wants us to be. Even if we had a compassion as large as his, we probably wouldn't make an impact on the world like he made, but we would make an impression on our neighborhood or our town for Jesus. Do you want to be pliable clay in your Master's hands? I pray that you do!

Perhaps you are thinking, "I do want God to use me in any way He sees fit. Can you tell me how I can become more pliable, less resistant, more responsive to the Lord's will for my life?" My answer is, "Yes! I can tell you how to become more responsive to His will. In order to do that I need to show you how He molds us. I need to discuss with you the tools He uses to shape us into the vessels of honor He wants us to be."

## *GOD'S TOOLS*

Tool number one is the Word. Consider what the Bible says on this subject. James 1:18 and I Peter 1:23 indicate that we are begotten by God through the word. We never could have been born again if the seed, the word, had not been planted in our hearts. Romans 10:17 says that faith comes through a hearing of the word of God. II Timothy 3:14-17 teaches that the Scriptures, the word, were inspired by God, and that they are able to make one who has studied them "wise unto salvation" and "thoroughly equipped for every kind of good work." Romans 12:2 challenges us to be transformed by the renewing of our minds, an exercise which involves saturating the mind with the word. Psalm 119:11 indicates that the word hidden in one's heart enables him to avoid sin against God. Verse 105 of that same Psalm says that the word lights our pathway. We could go on and on, but it should be obvious from these few references that God uses the word to shape us, to transform us into the people He wants us to be.

It is the word which *informs* us of the truth about God and His

Son, Jesus. It becomes, therefore, the basis of our faith (Rom. 10:13-14,17). The word *inspires* us with the story of Jesus, His miraculous birth, His wonderful teaching, His marvelous compassion, His mighty power, His magnificent demonstration of love on the cross of Calvary, and His glorious resurrection and ascension into heaven. That Gospel message convinces us of God's goodness and makes us ashamed of our own sinful lives. Those two things lead us to repentance (Rom. 2:4 and II Cor. 7:10). The word *instructs* us. It gives us directions as to how we can accept the pardon Jesus offers us and as to what we must do to remain faithful to Him until the end.

If we want to be responsive to the Master's touch, if we want to take on the shape and design He desires in us, it behoves us to study the word. II Timothy 2:15 admonishes us to study that we might win God's approval. In order for the word to have maximum influence on us, we must read it daily, memorize key passages and internalize its message. We must so saturate our minds with the word that it becomes a part of our reasoning process. Every decision will then be influenced by what the word has taught us God's will is.

Psalm 1 describes the man of God as one whose delight is in the Law of the Lord, and it indicates that he meditates on it day and night. Let me give you a simple, practical suggestion as to how you can keep the word of God on your mind at all times. Have you ever had a tune to stick in your mind? Do you find yourself humming it or singing it over and over again? Most of us have done that countless times. Did you know that some of the most talented Christian song writers today are writing what they call "Scripture songs?" They are putting the words of scripture to music. Many of the tunes are catchy. They stick in your mind. My advice is that you learn as many of these Scripture songs as you can. Then let their messages surface in your mind all through your days. You will find you really are meditating on the word day and night. You will also discover that God is shaping you and your attitudes through His word.

## *CIRCUMSTANCES*

The second tool God uses to shape our lives is circumstances. Often they seem to be adverse ones. Think about two very prominent Old Testament characters, Moses and Joseph. You know their stories. They are familiar to everyone who has spent much time in Sunday School. Their experiences were similar. Both were brought up as favorites, given every luxury their doting parents could provide. Joseph, raised in the tents of his wealthy, nomadic chieftan father, had an exaggerated idea of his own importance because he was favored over his brothers. Moses, brought up in Pharaoh's household and trained in all the wisdom of Egypt, thought the Israelites ought to recognize him automatically as their leader and deliverer (see Acts 7:25). God used the circumstances in each of those cases to prepare the men for leadership. At that point in their lives they had all the confidence one needs to assume a position of command, but they lacked one requirement which is essential in anyone who would be a leader for God. They lacked humility. The Lord used adverse circumstances to instill that quality in each of them. Joseph's brothers sold him as a slave. That experience along with a false accusation which landed him in prison convinced him that he was as totally dependent on God as everyone else. It taught him humility as nothing else could have. Moses had to flee from Egypt when it became known that he had killed an Egyptian. For forty years he lived in Midian. All of the leadership skills he had developed were put on the shelf as he kept his father-in-law's sheep. When he had learned his lesson in humility, God made him the greatest leader the world had ever known.

Another Old Testament personality who was shaped by circumstances into a vessel of honor for God was Hosea. He learned from bitter experience what it was like to love someone who was unfaithful. His wife, Gomer, ran away with her lovers and disgraced herself and her husband. But Hosea still loved her. When he found her one day on the slave block, he bought her back and took her home. He learned that the price of forgiveness is often high, and that one who loves is willing to pay the price. Hosea's message to Israel then became a message of God's love. The nation had been unfaithful. She had forsaken God to go wantonly after idols, but God's love for her never faltered. He wanted her back. He was willing to pay the price to forgive her. For the first time, a prophet understood something of the heartbreak God was experiencing because of His people's unfaithfulness. God used Hosea's own tragic home life to teach His people about His love. Hosea was shaped by his circumstances into what God wanted him to be.

There is another side to this story. If we rebel, if we become bitter when adverse circumstances strike us, we can prevent God's plans for us from being carried out. Merrill Womack was horribly burned in a plane crash. His face could be called monstrous except for the fact that there is a light in his eyes, a lilt in his voice and a smile on his lips. He is a magnificent testimony to the fact that God can give anyone peace and joy. He could have become bitter. He could have spent his life moping and feeling sorry for himself and making everyone around him miserable. God would have wept because He wanted to bless people's lives with his wonderful testimony. Merrill Womack thanks God for that accident because he knows he is a better man today; he has a greater faith; and he has been a blessing to many more people than he could have been without it.

So, I would say to you, "Rejoice in adversity or in prosperity." God intends for all your circumstances to help shape you into a vessel which will honor His name.

## *PEOPLE*

Let me point out, finally, that God also uses people to mold us according to His will. Consider the statement of Acts 4:13. The council of the Jews had called Peter and John to task for preaching through Jesus the resurrection of the dead. They demanded to know by what authority or in what name they had healed the lame man. Peter responded with magnificent audacity. He announced the Lordship of Jesus, proclaimed His resurrection and laid the blame for His crucifixion at the feet of the council. Is it any wonder they marvelled when they saw the boldness of Peter and John? Now, look at what they noted about them: "They had been with Jesus." You see, they recognized that the apostles had been shaped by their contact with Jesus. You and I can also be shaped by contact with the Lord if we will spend extended periods of time with Him in prayer.

Other people influence our lives also. Consider Philippians 2:19-23. Paul there gives Timothy a rich commendation. He tells the Philippians he has "no man like minded who will naturally care for your state." He went on to remind them that they knew Timothy had served along side of him in proclaiming the gospel like a son with his father. Timothy had become the man he was because of the influence Paul had in his life. It was not the only influence, of course. Timothy's mother and grandmother had also had a positive impact on his life (see II Tim. 1:5).

My own life has taken on the shape it has because of certain key people. My parents gave me a wonderful example. They loved each other and their children. They each had a strong desire to be pleasing to the Lord and a blessing to others. I often fail to live up to the example they provided, but I have no doubt that I am what I am today largely because of their influence. Perhaps even more, my wife Diane has helped me take on the shape God wants me to have. Her cooking has enlarged my girth considerably. She has taught me patience in adversity. I shouldn't write those things when she has no chance at rebuttal. Seriously, Diane has a wonderful sensitivity to people and their needs. She has great wisdom in dealing with people and a deep sincerity of desire to please God. She has kept me from doing many foolish things and has helped me immeasurably in my quest to become the man God wants me to be.

You know who the people are who have been used by God to shape your life. You also know of people who may have been used by the devil to lead you to rebel against some aspect of God's plan for your life. I urge you to choose your companions very carefully. Spend as much time as you can with people who will help you grow in the Lord. Don't allow even those who are nearest and dearest to you to slow you down or turn you from the path He has mapped out for you.

Of course, you know, influence is reciprocal. You also have an impact on those who come into contact with you. Pray for strength and guidance that you may help to shape them into the vessels God wants them to be.

## *CONCLUSION*

Let me conclude this chapter by pointing out that it takes a great deal of effort for stubborn, rebellious human beings to yield themselves to the Lord as clay in the Potter's hands. It takes prayer and study and repentance and faith, and all of those things require self-discipline. It isn't easy to set aside a period of time each day for Bible study and prayer. It takes self-discipline to keep on praying day after day even when we are discouraged. It takes courage to say the things we need to say to friends and loved ones to point them in the direction the Lord would have them travel.It takes great courage to reject the counsel of a loved one when you know God has a different plan for you. It hurts when people criticize you for being fanatical because you cling to your convictions. Are you willing to face all those things and more because you really want to be finest vessel God can make of you, a vessel which will bring glory and honor to the Master Potter?

## Discussion Questions

1. Since God is the ruler of the universe, why do we need to pray that His will be done in our lives?

2. Can you think of other tools God uses to mold our lives? (That is, other than the Word, Circumstances and People.)

3. If a person spoils God's plan for his life by resisting the Lord's will, is it possible for him to undo his mistakes and yet be made into a vessel of surpassing loveliness? Is it likely that it will be what God originally planned?

4. Can you think of incidents in your own life when adverse circumstances gave God an opportunity to increase your faith and your usefulness to His kingdom?

5. Children often adopt the attitudes of their parents even more than they imitate their actions. Can you think of some attitudes you need to change for the benefit of your children or others whose lives you influence?

6. Who has had the greatest influence in molding your life? Has it been to the glory of God? Think of some people who have had an impact on your life and thank God for those who have influenced you for good.

## Chapter Seven
# DAILY BREAD

The word translated "daily" in Matthew 6:11 is a very rare word in our New Testaments. It is found only there and in Luke's version of the Lord's Prayer. Scholars are uncertain as to its meaning. Perhaps the best translation would be "sufficient." If that is correct, then we would be praying, "Give us this day sufficient bread to sustain us today." J.B. Phillips translates it, "Give us this day the bread we need."

With this petition the Lord made a transition from requests which have to do with the glory and honor of God to those which deal with the needs of men. We would do well at this point to observe again the sequence of these petitions, for as we have seen before, they teach us something about our priorities.

The first three petitions have to do with God's glory, His kingdom, and His will. That is as it should be. Our most ardent desires should be that His name be held sacred, His kingdom be established in the hearts of men, and His will be done as eagerly and as thoroughly on earth as it is in heaven. Perhaps you have noticed that those petitions proceed from the inward to the outward, that they have to do with the heart, the will and the actions of men. Again, that is as it should be. It is the natural order of progression with human beings. When the heart is right, it will bring the will into position and produce the proper actions. When He was asked, "Which is the great commandment?" Jesus replied, "Thou shalt love the Lord thy God with all thy heart, and with all thy soul, and with all thy mind. This is the first and great commandment." In Luke 6:45 He explained why it is of primary importance to have the heart right, "A good man out of the good treasure of his heart bringeth forth that which is good; and an evil man out of the evil treasure of his heart bringeth forth that which is evil." When a man loves God with his whole heart, he will surrender his will completely to the Lord's will. Romans 2:4 assures us that the goodness of God is meant to produce repentance in us and II Corinthians 7:10 says that Godly sorrow brings forth repentance. When we see how good God is and how sinful we are, it makes us ashamed and our hearts reach out in love to the One who loves us so much. That is repentance. It is the decision to crucify self and allow Him to take over our lives, to live in us. It is the decision to make Him our King, to become His subject, to establish His kingdom within us. Once that decision is made, our actions are brought into conformity with His will. We are eager to do it. Jesus arranged the first three petitions of His prayer in accordance with the natural progression from love of God to surrender of the will to overt action. When we love God with the whole heart, our greatest desire is that His name be honored among all men. When we love Him with the whole mind, we submit our wills totally to Him. When we love Him with our whole soul (the word for soul means "life") we do His bidding in every area of our lives.

Beginning with the fourth petition of this prayer, the emphasis shifts from the glorifying of God to dealing with the needs of men. Here again, the order is significant. It proceeds from man's simplest needs to his most profound ones, from sustenance for the body to cleansing for the soul and elevation of the spirit. Again, this is as it must be. The physical must be dealt with first. We are spiritual beings dwelling in physical bodies. Man does not live by bread alone, but he must have bread to survive. He can not nourish the spirit unless he is alive, and before he can conquer sin and self, he must have the burden of guilt lifted from his soul by the forgiveness of God. Therefore, Jesus taught us to pray in the proper order: for bread, for forgiveness, and for victory over self and sin.

## *THE REQUEST FOR BREAD*

In this chapter we will consider the first in this second class of petitions, the request for bread. I believe Jesus meant for us to understand it to be a request for all those things which we need to sustain our lives. We will consider its implications in regard to proper attitudes and actions as well as its teaching concerning prayer.

First of all, we need to notice that this request for bread implies that we are dependent upon God to satisfy even our simplest needs. The scriptures state that very clearly in other places. Acts 17:25 says that He gives us life and breath and all things. Then in verse 28 of that same chapter it says that we live, and move, and have our being in Him. Hebrews 1:3 informs us that He upholds all things by the word of His power, and Colossians 1:17 says that all things "hold together" in Him. "Hold together" is a literal translation of the word translated "consist" in the King James Version.

This statement of Paul, "by Him all things hold together," has special significance in a scientific age. We know all matter is made up of atoms and those atoms are joined together to form solids and liquids by some force science doesn't understand. We get an idea of just how powerful that force is when atoms are split — an atomic explosion occurs. That power which holds everything together is provided by God.

It is God who keeps the sun shining in the heavens. It is God who keeps the atmosphere in a delicate balance so the oxygen in that atmosphere sustains our lives. We have no control over it. God created and sustains the atmosphere. We simply enjoy it. We could not live another instant without Him, and I think Jesus taught us to pray, "Give us this day the bread we need to sustain our lives" in order to remind us that we depend on Him for everything.

It may seem strange to ask God for what we already have. Most of our homes have plenty of food in them for today and many days to come. But when we pray that prayer, we acknowledge our total dependence on Him. We say to Him, "We realize we need You every hour. We could not live at all without Your blessings. In You we 'live and move and have our being.' " Our Father doesn't need our praise as an ego booster, but He does appreciate it because praise demonstrates that our attitudes are what they should be.

In addition, asking for daily bread reminds *us* that He is the source of every blessing, and we need that reminder. It is so easy to forget how much we need Him when we are enjoying great prosperity. In the midst of hardships and difficulties, when we can't seem to help ourselves, we don't need any reminders of our dependence on Him. But when everything seems to be going right, we tend to forget Who makes it that way. This prayer is one way of keeping our minds focused on the Source of our blessings.

## *PROPER ATTITUDES TOWARD MATERIAL THINGS*

In Matthew 6:19-34 Jesus dealt at length with the proper attitudes toward material things. He indicated that we should not try to achieve a feeling of security by laying up wealth on earth. He reminded us that material things are subject to decay and other kinds of destruction; that those who have material wealth may suddenly find themselves in poverty. We should make sure we treasure most the things of heaven. We should set our hearts on those things, then we won't be disappointed. Citizens of Cambodia and other war torn lands could tell us just how precarious material wealth really is. A news article I read recently told about some of the richest people in America. It quoted Carolyn Hunt, a billionaire, as saying she has always been afraid she would one day be penniless. That ought to say to us very clearly that there is no security in material wealth. Don't try to gain a feeling of security by amassing wealth. It won't work. You can't get enough of it to make you feel you have nothing to worry about. The only security is in God, through trusting Him. It is only when we can say with David, "The Lord is my shepherd, I shall not want," that we can experience real security.

In verses 25 and 26 Jesus taught us not to worry about the necessities, food, drink and clothing. In verse 33 He indicated that we should make citizenship in His kingdom and the attainment of righteousness the goals upon which we set our hearts. When we do that, God will provide all the things we need.

We should take special note of verse 26. By using the fowl of the air as an example, He taught a very important truth, that is, God feeds the birds daily, but they don't worry about it. However, they do have to search for their food. They have to work to provide for themselves and their offspring. Just so, God gives us the strength, ability and opportunity and expects us to perform the necessary labor to provide for our families.

In verse 24 He dealt with motivation. We must work to provide for those under our care, but we must not allow our hearts to become enamored with material things. We must remember who our Master is; we must remember whom we serve. We must not set our hearts on material things, for if we think things will satisfy our deepest longings and we bend every effort to acquire them, mammon will have become our master, our god. We will have to despise the Lord and His teachings in order to pursue our goals. The first thing you know, we will be neglecting our tithe so we can purchase some thing we think will make us happy. Then, perhaps we will cheat on our income tax. There is no end. If we love material things, mammon will become our god, and we can't have two. We can't serve God and mammon.

Now, it may seem like a paradox, but the proper attitude toward God eliminates anxiety about the supply of our needs and allows us to give ourselves whole heartedly to our work. When God put Adam and Eve out of the Garden of Eden, He told Adam he would have to earn his living. "In the sweat of your face," He said, "you shall eat bread" (Gen.3:19). Therefore, we know work is ordained of God, so we can do our work "heartily, as to the Lord and not unto men" (Col.3:23).

In verses 28-30 Jesus said something about luxuries. For all of our anxiety about appearance, we can not produce a beauty which even approaches what God provides. He teaches us to ask for the necessities and to be satisfied when we receive them. He wants us to concentrate our efforts on making Him our king and on conforming our lives to His blessed example that we may be acceptable before Him. When we have done that, He will give us a beauty that is neither fragile or transcient.

Consider these words of scripture: "Having food and raiment let us be therewith content" (I Tim. 6:8). "Be content with such things as ye have" (Heb. 13:5). "For I have learned, in whatever state I am, therewith to be content. I know both how to be abased, and I know how to abound: everywhere and in all things I am instructed both to be full and to be hungry, both to abound and to suffer need. I can do all things through Christ which strengtheneth me" (Phil. 4:11-13). Since he said that, it is no wonder Paul would say, "Godliness with contentment is great gain" (I Tim. 6:6).

To be adorned with the kind of character which is never bitter, always rejoicing, always blessing others is to have a beauty which will go on into eternity. Haven't you seen elderly people who have grown old in the Lord, who spend their days blessing others? They always have a kind word, a warm smile for you and everyone else. Their faces radiate the love in their hearts. There is nothing more beautiful on this earth than a godly old person unless it is a tiny baby, and both were made by God.

One other thing I want to point out concerning asking God for the necessities. He knows we would also like to have some of the luxuries others enjoy. But what we want is not always good for us. If it is, He is "able to do exceedingly abundantly above all that we ask or think." When He does grant those blessings, it is proper to rejoice and praise Him for His kindness. It is, however, of utmost importance that we minimize the desire for material things, for if we allow that desire to become strong, it can lead to all kinds of activities which will not please our Lord. I Timothy 6:9 states the case very clearly, "They that will be rich fall into temptation and a snare, and into many foolish and hurtful lusts which drown men in destruction and perdition." The desire for riches leads men into unscrupulous practices. We must always remember that it is far better to poor, to have less than those around us, to be in actual need than to cheat or abuse someone else in the attempt to grow rich. Perhaps more to the point for the average Christian, we must guard against the sins of envy and greed. We must not allow money matters to make us bitter or sullen. We must set our affections on those things which money can not purchase: loving families, meaningful lives, a close relationship with the Lord. Godliness with contentment is great gain!

## *PRAYING IN THE PLURAL*

Now, please notice that this petition, "Give us this day our daily bread," and all those which follow it in the Lord's Prayer are stated in the plural. Jesus never once used "me" or "my" in teaching us to pray. He intended for us to consider ourselves individual members of the whole which is mankind. He wanted us to plead for all of our brothers and sisters as well as for ourselves.

In a land of plenty most of us have never been really hungry. Oh, we have known stomach hunger. Once our stomachs get empty we begin to feel pangs. Sometimes our inward parts even make audible protests when they aren't given the food they want at the usual time. That's not the kind of hunger I am referring to. I mean tissue hunger. Try this: (If you don't have diabetes or some other physical condition which forbids it.) Fast for four days. About the third day you will notice you aren't hungry any more. Your body has shifted gears. It has gotten into the groove of converting fat into energy. Once that process is working efficiently, if you continue fasting, you won't feel any real hunger again until all your fat has been consumed. They tell me it takes about six weeks. At that point your body begins to convert muscle tissue into energy. Then you will feel the kind of hunger most of us have never experienced. It is the point at which you begin to die of starvation. That is tissue hunger. Most Americans have never felt it, but half of the people of the world have. For them it is a way of life. Think of that when you pray, "Give us this day our daily bread." Then you will be praying not just for your own sustenance, but for the needs of your brothers and sisters everywhere. That is the way Jesus would have us to pray.

Of course, if we pray like that, it behoves us to do something else. We must share the abundance He has given us to help relieve the suffering of our brothers and sisters in other parts of the world. A study reported in the June, 1986, issue of the *American Journal of Public Health* gave some startling statistics. It indicated that Americans spent 250 times as much for the service of prostitutes as they gave to foreign mission work. They spent 10 times as much for soft drinks, and slightly more for chewing gum. They also gave more than 20 times as much for church work at home as they gave to their brothers and sisters overseas. The report had to do with statistics for 1913. Do you think the percentages have changed since then. Our society is certainly not more righteous now than it was then.

It is very difficult to be content with just food and clothing in America, but surely we should be willing to give up a few of the luxuries so others could have something to eat. Think about it, then do something even if it isn't very much. Do something!

## Discussion Questions

1. Discuss the significance of the idea of praying for the sustenance we need for survival in the light of the fact that Jesus lived in deep poverty, owning only the clothes on His back.

2. Why should we pray for the food we need for today when our cupboards are well stocked with food?

3. Why do you think Jesus taught us to make our petitions in the plural, never asking for any blessing just for ourselves as individuals?

4. Since man does not live by bread alone, why do you think Jesus gave us instructions to pray for physical sustenance before praying for cleansing for the soul and elevation of the spirit?

5. How can you reconcile the following ideas: That we must eliminate anxiety about our needs by trusting God to supply them, that we should pray for our needs to be fulfilled, and that we should do our work to provide for our households "heartily as unto the Lord?"

6. When we pray that the daily bread of our brothers and sisters in the third world countries be supplied, that obviously obligates us to do what we can to help supply that bread. How far does that obligation go? At what point can we say we have done all the Lord wants us to do in providing for them?

## Chapter Eight

# FORGIVE US OUR DEBTS

Prayer, to be all that Jesus intended it to be, must include asking for blessings for ourselves and others. We must seek first the honor and glory of His name. We must seek that first, but not exclusively. Our Father delights to have His children recognize Him as the giver of every good and perfect gift. He also delights to lavish those gifts upon us. Nothing pleases Him more than to have His children come to Him humbly asking that He supply their needs. After all, He did say, "Ask and it shall be given you; seek, and ye shall find, knock, and it shall be opened unto you: for everyone that asketh receiveth; and he that seeketh findeth; and to him that knocketh, it shall be opened" (Matt. 7:7,8).

In a few brief words our Lord taught us how to ask for the very things which are essential for our well being. He taught us to ask for those things which are necessary for our physical sustenance with the words, "Give us this day our daily bread." I think He meant for us to understand that we were to ask for more than just food. We should ask for clothing, shelter, health, and life itself (see Matt. 6:28-30). He wants us to realize we cannot provide anything for ourselves. It is He who gives us the strength, intelligence, ability, talent, and opportunity to earn our livings. So, even though we must work to earn the necessities, it is He who supplies them. When we ask Him to supply, we are asking for the opportunity to earn and the capability to do whatever job we must to secure what we need for ourselves and our families. When we seek first His kingdom and His righteousness, He will provide all we need.

Jesus taught us to ask for the one thing we need most for mental health and stability with the words, "Forgive us our debts as we forgive our debtors." Depression, despondency, paranoia and most other forms of mental illness stem from guilt, from our recognition of the wide gap between what we are and what we should and could be. Jesus knew the only way to deal with our guilt was through forgiveness. When God forgives our sins, the burden of guilt is removed. Then, when we understand that His love for us is unconditional and uninterrupted and that His willingness to forgive us when we repent is inexhaustible, we know we have found the perfect answer to our problem of guilt. Of course, our weakness and our continuing susceptibility to sin must also be handled. He had the answer for that, too. He taught us to pray, "Lead us not into temptation, but deliver us from evil." When God answers the four simple petitions Jesus taught us in the Lord's Prayer, He provides all we need for our physical, mental and spiritual well being. When we learn to pray as He wanted us to pray, we will be close to becoming the people our Lord wants us to be.

In this chapter we will examine the concepts in the request,"Forgive us our debts." We will seek the answers to three questions: 1. What did He mean by "debts" and the other words He used when He spoke of forgiveness? 2. How should we go about asking for forgiveness? and 3. What should we do if we feel no real sense of guilt?

## *THE WORDS HE USED*

In Matthew 6:12 Jesus used the word "debts" in reference to our guilt. That word carries the idea of something owed to another, something which is his rightful due. An employer, for example, is in debt to his employee until he pays him the wages he is due. Paul wrote in Romans 13:7-8, "Render therefore to all their dues: tribute to whom tribute is due: custom to whom custom; fear to whom fear; honour to whom honour. Owe no man anything, but to love one another." From that passage it is obvious that a debt can be other than monetary. We owe honor and respect to our parents and will be in debt to them unless we pay up. Paul also indicated that he was a debtor to all men, to the cultured and the ignorant, to the wise and unwise. He had a message to share with all mankind. He owed it to all men to share it with them. He was obligated. He would have failed in his responsibility if he had not preached it to everyone who would listen.

Jesus was teaching us to ask God to forgive us for those times when we fail to pay Him what He is due. We owe Him reverence, obedience and love. We are in debt to Him because of the countless times we have neglected to honor and praise Him. When we pray, "Forgive us our debts," we are saying, "Lord, please don't hold those failures against us. We intend to honor and obey You always, but sometimes we fail. We forget to trust You completely. Please don't reject us. Please give us another chance."

Jesus developed the concept of debts in the parable found in Matthew 18:21-35. Peter had asked if they should go so far as to forgive a brother seven times. The rabbis taught that to forgive three times fulfilled one's responsibility. Peter was being generous, far more generous than most of us. Suppose a brother cheated you, would you give him another chance? Suppose he came to you asking for forgiveness, would you grant it and trust him again? I mean really trust him! Would you do it seven times? That's what Peter suggested. But you know what Jesus answered don't you? Not seven times, but seventy times seven. That's 490 times. I can't imagine anyone seeking forgiveness that many times. Can you? That's the point. Jesus was saying, "No matter how many times they offend you, keep on forgiving."

That is the background for this parable. Jesus tells of a king who called his servant to account. One was brought before him who owed 10,000 talents. When he could not pay, he begged for time. The Master, moved with compassion, completely forgave the debt. The servant then went out from his Master's presence and accosted a fellow servant who owed him 100 pence. The man could not pay and asked for time using the very same words he, himself, had used in pleading with his Master, but the request was denied. He had that fellow servant cast into debtor's prison. When the king heard of his servant's hard heartedness, he called him back, rebuked him and turned him over to the tormentors.

Now, let me point out some things which may not be obvious to the reader of English versions of the New Testament. First of all, the talent was the largest denomination of their money. To owe someone one talent would have been an impossible debt for the common man. Jesus evidently was indicating that every sin is a major one, every sin puts us in debt to God in a big way. They may seem insignificant to us if they "hurt no one but ourselves," but they are grievous to our Father. Each one is an expression of our unwillingness to obey Him.

One the other hand, 100 pence is a very small debt. Anyone, given time, could pay it back. Jesus was teaching that the offences we commit against each other, though they may be terrible, can not compare with our nearly uninterrupted rebellion against the Father's loving administration. Those offenses against the Father's love are continuous, the very state in which we live.

Finally, the total of 10,000 talents is an overwhelming sum. In our money it would amount to more than $20 million. The man couldn't have made a significant dent in that debt with a lifetime of labor. Jesus meant to teach us that we can not hope to pay off our debts to Him. A lifetime of service could not erase the sins of our past. They can only be removed by His forgiveness.

The second word Jesus used to refer to our guilt was "trespasses" (Matt. 6:14,15). The Greek word originally referred to a false step and, therefore, to an overstepping of our authority, an intrusion onto someone else's territory. It is translated in several different ways in the King James Version of the New Testament. Each of them is appropriate.

In Ephesians 1:7 and Colossians 2:13, it is "sin." To intrude onto God's territory, His authority, is sin. In James 5:16 and Galatians 6:1 it is "faults." One of our most grievous faults is our tendency to overstep our authority. It is "offences" in Romans 4:25 and 5:15,16. It almost always offends others when we trespass onto their authority.

All sin is an overstepping of our authority, an intrusion into God's realm. It is pushing Him aside and placing ourselves on His throne so we can make our own rules or set His aside so they don't apply to us. In short, sin is rebellion against His authority and going about to set up our own. We don't like His rules. We think we can't be happy if we have to keep them all the time. We rebel against Him because we just can't bring ourselves to trust Him completely.

A man says, for example, "I know I ought to give a tithe, but I just can't afford to right now. As soon as some of my bills are paid off I'll start." His problem is that he can't bring himself to trust God to make 90% of his income go farther than 100% does. So, he thinks the rules should not apply to him. It doesn't matter that God made the rules. He doesn't trust the Lord to make them work for him.

Another example, a woman says, "I know I shouldn't watch those filthy soap operas. They are full of illicit sex and all kinds of unwholesome things I shouldn't be thinking about, but I've just got to have some kind of diversion. The kids are driving me nuts. I can't afford to hire a baby sitter whenever the notion strikes. I can sit down for a few minutes while the baby is sleeping and watch one of my programs and it relaxes me." She is saying that God doesn't understand her circumstances or that He does and He will allow this relaxing of the rules for her. Again, she needs to realize that God made His rules perfect. He has the correct solution to her problem. She needs to trust Him to enable her to deal with that problem without resorting to the devil's solution. She has no right to set aside God's rules. When she does, she is pushing Him off the throne and establishing herself there. She is trespassing on His territory, and she needs to ask him to forgive her.

When millions of mothers in America make the decision to end the lives of their unborn children, they are assuming the role of God in a most alarming way. One must play the part of God to decide when another human being ought to die. An abortion is not simply the "termination of a pregnancy." It is the ending of a life. God makes the decision to allow a life to begin and only He has the right to decide when one should end.

When we seek the forgiveness of our trespasses, we are asking God to forgive our intrusions into His territory. We are asking Him to take back the throne of our lives, to reassume that role as we submit once again to His authority. It should be a foregone conclusion that we would never intentionally push Him off the throne again.

The third word Jesus used to refer to our guilt is found in Luke 11:4. It is translated "sins." The Greek is *Hamartias*. It means "a failure." The verb form means, "to miss the mark." It is the offense of a servant. Entrusted with certain responsibilities, he fails to measure up, fails to perform up to the standard expected.

Our standard is Jesus. We are told that he left us "an example that (we) should follow His steps" (I Peter 2:21). We should seek to be as loving, as compassionate, as self giving, as obedient to the Father's will, as patient and as faithful as Jesus. Of course, we will never live up to that standard, we will always miss the mark. So, it will always be necessary for us to pray, "Forgive us our sins."

## *THE RIGHT WAY TO SEEK FORGIVENESS*

We need to see now the way we should approach God to plead for mercy. Two things are necessary as we come to the Lord with this petition. First, we must overcome self righteousness and pride, and then we must just ask to be forgiven. It is assumed that we will be determined to avoid the same pitfalls which have laid us low in the past.

To seek forgiveness from God, one must first have a keen sense of his guilt. We must recognize, acknowledge, and accept our sinfulness before we will be inclined to ask forgiveness. Sometimes a Christian compares himself with worldly people and begins to feel rather proud of himself. He sees that he does not commit those gross sins of his neighbors. He doesn't get drunk, beat his wife, or kick the cat. He does not watch filth on T.V. or read pornographic magazines. He has never killed anyone. He doesn't steal. He pays his debts, doesn't cheat on his income tax. So far as he knows, he has never slandered anyone. He is faithful to his wife. So why should he seek forgiveness? What has he done wrong?

The problem when we begin to think like that is that we are using the wrong standard of comparison, the wrong criteria of judgment. Instead of looking at our neighbors, we need to look at Jesus and His teachings. If you don't feel very guilty, you need to pick up the Bible and begin to read. See what it requires of us, and you'll begin to see how far you are from being the person you ought to be.

Here are just a few of the ways in which I dare say all of us fail:

"Love your enemies, bless them that curse you, do good to them that hate you, and pray for them which despitefully use you, and persecute you" (Matt. 5:44). Do you obey those commands of Jesus? Have you had anyone to "cuss you out" lately? Did you bless him in return? (To bless means "to speak well of.") Did you find something good about that person who cursed you and say something meant to build him up? Has someone taken advantage of you recently, despitefully used you? Did you pray for him? Did you return good for evil? That's what Jesus said His followers would do. Do you begin to see why you should feel guilty before God?

Consider the beatitudes. Are you humble? Do you weep over your failure to be the person you ought to be? Are you totally surrendered to the Father? Are you hungry and thirsty for righteousness? Are you merciful and generous toward others? Are your motives pure and holy? Are you actively seeking to lead men to peace with God? Are you faithful to the point of suffering for Him?

Look at I Corinthians 13:4-7. It is Paul's description of the love every Christian is to live.

> Love is patient and kind; love is not jealous or boastful; it is not arrogant or rude. Love does not insist on its way, it is not irritable or resentful; it does not rejoice at wrong, but rejoices in the right. Love bears all things, believes all things, hopes all things, endures all things.

Does that describe you? Are you never irritable or resentful? Never arrogant or rude? Always patient and kind? Never insist on your own way? If we will only read the word of God and compare ourselves with Jesus, we will never have any problem with self righteousness. We will always see how very sinful we are. We will feel a great need to seek forgiveness.

## *ATTITUDES TOWARD OTHERS*

A deep sense of guilt before God is only one of the attitudes we need as we seek His mercy. A second problem may be our attitudes toward others. We are told that the merciful will receive mercy. We must be as forgiving and generous toward others as we desire God to be toward us. We must not hold it against them when they fail to pay us the respect or honor we believe is our due. When they don't give us credit for our accomplishments or appreciate what we do for them, we must harbor no resentment against them, but must freely forgive them those debts. We must not retaliate when they intrude onto our authority or push us aside to usurp our responsibilities. When they perform badly and we get the blame, we must return good for evil. When others fail to perform according to the standards we have set up for them, we must in kindness and mercy love them anyway. In short, we must forgive if we wish to be forgiven.

It will not be difficult to forgive others if we have the proper attitude toward ourselves. Paul spoke of himself as "the chief" of sinners, I Timothy 1:15, and "less than the least of all saints"(Eph. 3:8). He did not say he *was* the chief of sinners in the past. He said, "I am chief." Evidently he still considered himself a sinner of the worst kind at the time he wrote his first letter to Timothy. When one has an acute awareness of his own unworthiness, he won't look down on other sinners. He will feel compassion and mercy toward them. So cultivate that sense of unworthiness. It will enable you to approach God with the proper spirit to seek His forgiveness.

## *CONFESSION AND FORGIVENESS*

When we have our attitudes right, only one thing remains. "If we confess our sins, he is faithful and just to forgive us our sins, and to cleanse us from all unrighteousness" (I John 1:9). You will notice it says sins, plural. We are to confess individual, specific sins. It is not enough just to repeat the words of Jesus, "Forgive us our debts." He was giving us an outline. We are to fill it in.

There will never be any great sense of guilt over vaguely defined debts. We must see specifically our offenses, our trespasses, and our failures to measure up. Then we can truly seek forgiveness. We are to pray like this: "Lord, I'm so sorry that I failed to encourage my preacher when he was feeling down. I didn't want to seem pushy. I was thinking of myself instead of him. Please forgive me and give me the strength to do the right thing the next time." Or, "Father, forgive me for repeating that gossip I heard. I wanted people to think more highly of me than they do of her, so I passed on the story about her weakness." Or, "Dear Lord, please forgive me for being so stingy. I know I should have been generous in my offering for that missionary, but I was more concerned about my own wants than the needs of those people who don't know Christ."

## *CONCLUSION*

Now let me conclude this chapter with a brief review. We have seen that we are all guilty before God. We are debtors to Him because we have failed to give Him what is due to Him. We have failed to give the reverence, praise, love and obedience He has a right to expect from us. We are trespassers because we have intruded onto His territory, we have usurped His authority. We have made ourselves kings in our own lives, pushed Him off the throne so we could make our own rules. We are sinners because we have missed the mark miserably. We have failed in our responsibilities, never quite performing up to the standard, Jesus.

We must humble ourselves and ask for forgiveness. We must recognize and admit our guilt. We must cultivate that sense of unworthiness, and realizing we are in no condition to condemn others, we must be as merciful and generous toward them as we desire God to be toward us.

We must confess our sins to God, naming them specifically with tears of regret and the determination to avoid those same pitfalls in the future. We must ask for His mercy. There is no other way to erase our guilt. A life time of service could not wipe out our prior offenses. Only God's forgiveness, His pardon, can do that.

All I have been saying here applies to Christians. If you are not a Christian, you must make up your mind to surrender to His will and commit your life to Him. Once you have demonstrated your willingness to obey Him in Christian baptism, and have completed that obedience, you will be a child of God, and these principles of forgiveness will apply to you.

One final note, we are not commanded to confess to any priest or any other representative of the Lord. We confess directly to Him in prayer.

## Discussion Questions

1. Some debts are not monetary in nature. What are some of the things we owe to our parents, teachers, spiritual leaders, government officials and to God?

2. Why is it so important to our mental wellbeing to be forgiven by God?

3. How do we "intrude on God's territory?"

4. What is the most significant difference between the offenses others commit against us and our offenses against God?

5. Why do some people feel very little sense of guilt? Why don't they feel any great need to seek God's forgiveness?

6. If a godly sorrow for sin is necessary before we can be forgiven, how can we feel that kind of sorrow without having a morbid, self-defeating grief that will stifle our effectiveness as servants of the Lord? How can we achieve a balance? How can we feel the sorrow that is necessary and yet feel the joy of one who has been forgiven?

## Chapter Nine
# AS WE FORGIVE OUR DEBTORS

There are seven petitions in the Lord's Prayer, seven different requests which Jesus taught us are appropriate to present to God in prayer. Only one of them was such that the Lord felt the need to explain it further. It is the one found in Matthew 6:12, "Forgive us our debts as we forgive our debtors." Verses 14 and 15 record the explanation. "For if ye forgive men their trespasses, your heavenly father will also forgive you, but if ye forgive not men their trespasses, neither will your father forgive your trespasses."

Those verses have presented a problem for many commentators because of their theology. They believe the only requirement for our salvation, the only thing that makes a man acceptable to God is faith. So, they have a problem with any passage which seems to require something other than faith. Now Jesus quite clearly taught that it is necessary for us to forgive if we are to continue receiving God's forgiveness. I don't see any other way to interpret this passage. Attempts to explain it some other way all seem to be straining to overcome its obvious meaning.

Arthur W. Pink is the one commentator I found who had some really helpful things to say on verses 14 and 15. I want to share with you two of the ideas he presented. First, we do not provide a pattern for God to follow in forgiving us. We are not asking Him to forgive us only to the degree we forgive others. Heaven forbid that it should be so. Our human forgiveness is never perfect. We often seem to retain just a tiny bit of resentment or vindictiveness. We never seem to be able to forget totally an offense which has been committed against us. But God's forgiveness is perfect. It provides a pattern for us to reach toward. So, when we pray, "forgive us our debts as we forgive our debtors," we do not mean to ask God to forgive us only to the degree we forgive others. We want that full gracious, loving pardon only He can give.

Second, we are reminding ourselves of a duty bound upon us. Whenever we ask for forgiveness, we ought always to add, "as we forgive our debtors."

We will discuss in this chapter the necessity of forgiveness, the scope of the forgiveness required of us, and the means of developing a forgiving heart.

## *FORGIVENESS REQUIRED*

Various passages of scripture teach that God requires those who are forgiven to forgive others. Look at the words of Jesus. The first indication from Him that we are required to forgive is found in this petition we are studying. Then the explanation in verses 14 and 15 should clear up any doubts we might have about forgiveness being required. "For if ye forgive men their trespasses, your heavenly father will also forgive you, but if ye forgive not men their trespasses, neither will your father forgive your trespasses." That's pretty straightforward. It's easy enough to understand. There is nothing obscure about it. Here are some other words of Jesus, "Blessed are the merciful, for they shall obtain mercy" (Matt. 5:7). When we are merciful to others, we receive the mercy of God. Look at Matthew 18:32-33, the parable of the unforgiving servant, when that servant was brought back before the Master after he had shown no mercy to a fellow servant. His Lord said to him, "O thou wicked servant, I forgave thee all that debt, because thou desiredst me; shouldest not thou also have had compassion on thy fellow servant?" We are told the Lord was angry with him and delivered him to the tormentors.

Now, I believe that refers to the tormentors in hell. It may also refer to torment here on earth. Charles Swindoll discusses this passage at length and says that when a person harbors bitterness and resentment in his heart, it torments him. Sourness in your spirit shows on your face. It etches lines that no amount of moisturing cream can ever erase.

In Ephesians 4:32 Paul said, "Be ye kind one to another, tender hearted, forgiving one another, even as God for Christ's sake hath forgiven you." There is that example held up before us again. As He forgave, we are to forgive. Then, perhaps the most pointed of all New Testament passages on this subject, James 2:13 "For judgment is without mercy to the one who has shown no mercy" (NKJV). It ought to be perfectly clear to anyone who will read the New Testament that the man who shows no mercy will receive none. Forgiveness is required. We must forgive if we want to continue receiving forgiveness. That is the plain teaching of scripture.

## *A BROAD RANGE OF FORGIVENESS REQUIRED*

Now, consider the scope of the forgiveness required of us. In the previous chapter I pointed out the three words Jesus used in reference to the offenses we commit: debts, trespasses, and sins. We ask to be forgiven of all of them, so we must also forgive them all.

Let's look at the idea of debts. We feel that people are indebted to us sometimes. Have you ever done something for someone and had him stab you in the back? You think, "After all I've done for him and he treats me like that." We feel they owe us something. That's a debt. We are to forgive our debtors. That's the only way to deal with it. Just freely forgive.

The severest tests of our Christianity often occur in our homes. There are many little irritations which we face at home, and sometimes we let them get us down. Let me illustrate it this way: A man comes home from work in the afternoon. It's been a tough day. He is thinking how nice it would be to come home, sit down in his favorite chair, pick up the newspaper and just leisurely browse through it, kind of unwind for a while. The first thing he wants to hear is, "Honey, supper is ready, come and eat." That's the way he pictures it in his mind. He hopes it will be that way, but it doesn't happen like that very often. At least it doesn't at my house. We have a seven-year-old daughter, and if I sit down to read the paper she may climb up in my lap and get between me and what I'm reading. Now, sometimes that irritates me. But, I remember the Bible says, "love is not irritable," and not "easily provoked," and I really do love her, so the best thing for me to do at that point is just lay aside my newspaper and give her my attention. That's all she wants, Daddy to love her and play with her, and that can be more relaxing and enjoyable than a newspaper. It's probably full of bad news anyway. On the other hand, sometimes you can get to thinking, "Why can't they give me a few minutes of peace and quiet after I've worked all day to make a living for them?" We think they owe us that. It's a debt. We pray, "Forgive us our debts as we forgive our debtors," so, we must forgive those debts.

Of course, it happens on the job too. Most of us can identify with Rodney Dangerfield and his trademark, "I don't get no respect." Probably all of us have felt that on the job at one time or another. We think, "Nobody appreciates me. After all the hours I put in trying to do the very best job I can do, it looks like someone would at least say, 'I appreciate what you're doing.' They owe me that." At least we feel like they do. But on most jobs you don't have people who come around and pat you on the back every now and then and say, "Boy, you're doing a terrific job." You don't get much of that. We would like to, but we don't. It is a wise manager or executive who does do some of that. He keeps his people happy. But most people don't get much appreciation expressed to them. We think we ought to. We feel they owe it to us, but we don't get it. So, forgive those who owe you something, your debtors. Just forgive them. They've got problems too.

Secondly, we need to think about forgiving trespasses. Let me give you another illustration from the home, because as I said, we face some of our severest tests there. I really believe it would be good for most of us to hang a plaque on our wall at home which has Ephesians 4:32 written on it to remind us of our need to be "kind to one another, tender hearted, forgiving one another, even as God for Christ's sake hath forgiven you." I know I need to be forgiven often, and probably you do too. I don't know of anything which would help make our homes happier than practicing Ephesians 4:32 in them. Here is the illustration: A man comes home from work in the afternoon, and his wife says, "Honey, could you stay with the kids for a little while? I need to run out to Wal-Mart." I don't know how it is at your house, but we have to go to Wal-Mart at least once a day. That's one of our things. We consider a day lost if we don't make at least one trip to Wal-Mart. Well, anyway, she asks you to stay with the kids for a little while, and you say, "Sure, go ahead. I'll be glad to keep the kids." Now again, if you have a seven-year-old, you know it is fun to play with them for about ten minutes. Then you run out of energy and they are just beginning to get wound up. You begin to think, "She said she would be gone just a few minutes. How much longer is she going to be?" Maybe she has been gone for more than an hour. You begin to wonder if she will ever come back. You think, "She's just using me. If she wanted to get away from the kids for a couple of hours, why didn't she say so?" Please don't think I'm accusing my wife of using me. She doesn't, but we can get to thinking that way sometimes even if it isn't true. What we need to do is just remember, "Forgive us as we forgive those who trespass against us." The only way to handle a situation like that is to forgive. Just as you need forgiveness, you must give it.

Then we ask forgiveness for our sins, so we also need to forgive those who sin against us. I think about this as something bigger than just little irritations like I've been talking about here. I know of a young woman who cannot remember her mother. The woman who gave birth to her died when she was quite small and her father remarried. The only mother she remembers is the stepmother who raised her. She loves her as the only mother she has ever known. Not long ago her father died. He left no will, but some years ago he deeded his property to his children. It was his intention that their stepmother would live in the home for the rest of her life, then they could do with it what they would. Within two weeks after his death, she sued her step children for the property. In the process of the litigation, she said to this young woman, her stepdaughter who had never known any other mother, "I never cared anything about you anyway." That would be tough. That would hurt deeply, but we are to forgive those who sin against us. That is the plain teaching of the Bible. We are to forgive. What they have done to us is not nearly so bad as what we've done to God. That stepmother trampled on the love of her stepdaughter, but we've done that to God. He continually reaches out to us in love and we turn away after the world. He forgives. "God commendeth his love toward us, in that, while we were yet sinners, Christ died for us." He did not wait for us to come to Him in repentance. He reached out to show us His love, to try to draw us back to Himself.

## *DEVELOPING A FORGIVING HEART*

How does one develop a forgiving heart? First of all, we need to meditate on what God has done for us. The forgiveness He has granted us is not a trivial thing. We will not appreciate that until we recognize the depth of our own unworthiness. There is a vast difference between saying, "I know I make mistakes. Everybody makes mistakes. Nobody is perfect," and saying, "I, Ed White, am a sinner. I'm guilty before God." There is a great deal of difference in the attitude which would lead someone to say, "Well, sure, I've told a few lies. Everybody has," and the attitude which produced these words from the apostle Paul, "O wretched man that I am! Who shall deliver me from the body of this death?" (Rom. 7:24). He was speaking as if a dead body had been strapped on his back and he couldn't get it off. Everywhere he went he was burdened down with the weight and stench of death on his back. That's how Paul viewed his own guilt. When Jesus said, "Blessed are they that mourn, for they shall be comforted" (Matt. 5:4), He was talking about people who mourn, who weep over the fact that they just cannot be as good as they want to be, as they know they ought to be. I tell you frankly, I don't believe anyone can be forgiven until he has a great thirst in his heart for the pardon of God. The Lord is pleased when we seek forgiveness not just to escape the penalty of sin, but because we desire the heart of our Father. Haven't you noticed that when you punish a child, he usually wants you to hold him, to comfort him, right after you've spanked him. It's because he wants to be assured that you still love him. That's what I want. I want my heavenly Father to say in effect, "It's all right son. I forgive you. I still love you." I'm not interested in just going through the proper channels to escape the horror of hell. I want more than that. I want my Father's heart.

We will not have a great thirst for the pardon of God until we have a keen sense of our own unworthiness. How could you or I ever be worthy of the love of One who allowed men to stretch out

His arms and drive great nails through His hands and feet, and hang Him up on a cross to die for us? When we understand how terribly unworthy we are, we can rejoice with exceeding great joy at the magnificent love of God, the grace that provides forgiveness for us in spite of ourselves. When we have an understanding of our own unworthiness, it will help us to be more generous in our attitudes toward others.

Then we need to consider the fact that we are slaves. Romans 6:16-18 says that we are the slaves of whomever we serve. If we serve sin, we are the slaves of sin. If we serve righteousness, we are the slaves of God. The King James Version says "servants," but the Greek word means slaves. We are His slaves, His property. We've been bought with a price (I Cor. 6:20). The price of our redemption was the precious blood of Jesus Christ.

There are some interesting facts about slaves. First, they don't own anything. Everything belongs to the Master. Second, they don't have any rights. Anything they are allowed to do is a privilege granted by the grace of their Master. Do you realize that most of the offenses which are committed against us have to do either with material possessions or what we consider to be our rights? Men cannot steal or destroy the treasures we have laid up in heaven. They can only do that with earthly things. They can't take away our standing with God, but they can destroy our prestige among men. It's when they take away our earthly treasures, or mess up our opportunities to advance, to make more money, and/or acquire greater prestige that we get angry and feel we've been cheated. When we realize we are slaves, that God controls our opportunities, provides our blessings, and looks out for our welfare, we won't get so upset about those things. We will be able to say with Joseph, "You thought evil against me; but God meant it unto good," (Gen.50:20-21) and we will be able to forgive and speak "kindly unto them" as he did. When we have the right attitude toward ourselves, the attitude of slaves, it is much easier to be forgiving toward others.

Thirdly, we need to put ourselves in their places. Jeanette

Williams' husband, Tom, was struck down by a car while on duty as a school crossing guard. The driver wasn't speeding or careless. She had been blinded by a low, glaring sun. But Jeanette was devastated. Tom was dead and she was alone. She knew she should forgive the woman, but she just couldn't seem to do it. Her preacher came by and talked with her about it. He said, "She's a teacher, she loves children, the way Tom did." He knew that unless Jeanette got that bitterness out of her heart, she would never have any peace. He wanted her to go see the woman.

She began to think about the other woman, tried to picture her in the classroom guiding, encouraging, concerned for her pupils. Then she sat down and asked God for the help she needed to forgive. He gave it to her the very next day. She did go see that woman, heard her say that she was afraid to drive now, that she couldn't work, couldn't eat. She put her arms around her and said, "I forgive you. Now you must forgive yourself."

It was when Jeanette Williams put herself in that other woman's shoes, when she began to realize how much it would hurt to be the one who had run over another human being, that she found the ability with God's help to forgive (*Guideposts*, Ap. 1982, pp. 14,15). God requires us to forgive. There is no question about it. There must be a heart of mercy and compassion in us if we expect to keep on receiving mercy and compassion from our heavenly Father.

## Discussion Questions

1. When God forgives us, He remembers our offenses no more. Is it required of us that we forget as well as forgive?

2. Discuss the various passages of scripture which show that God requires us to be merciful in order to keep on receiving His mercy and forgiveness.

3. What are some of the ways you feel that others are indebted to you? Do they sometimes fail to pay those debts? How should you feel toward them?

4. What scriptures can you list which give instructions about how you should deal with those who offend you? Do you find it difficult to comply with those instructions?

5. Can you think of other scriptures which, if practiced, would help make your relationship with others run smoothly?

6. How does it make you feel when you know you have done something to offend a friend and he forgives you graciously and completely?

7. Do you sometimes find it difficult to forgive yourself? Do you morbidly keep dwelling on your failures? Do you think God would have you forget them and move on so you can be a positive, productive servant? Or do you think He would have you retain a strong memory of your failure so it can be a deterrent in the future?

## Chapter Ten
# LEAD US NOT INTO TEMPTATION

The Bible can be confusing. Sometimes the teachings of one passage seem to conflict with those of another. For example, James says (1:2) we should "count it all joy when (we) fall into divers temptations," but Jesus taught us to pray "lead us not into temptation." James also says that God does not tempt anyone, (James 1:13) but Matthew tells us that Jesus was "Led up of the spirit into the wilderness to be tempted of the devil" (Matt. 4:1). Now, if the spirit of God led Jesus into the wilderness to be tempted, surely He was responsible for the temptation in some sense. And why would Jesus teach us to pray "lead us not into temptation" if He was led into it?

I believe the answers to these perplexing questions can be

found in considering two things. First, the word translated "temptations" should be rendered "trials" or "tests" in some places. We will look at the difference in a moment. Second, an understanding of our Lord's use of the phrase "into temptation" will help clear up the supposed contradiction.

Now let's look at the difference between trials and temptations. The two terms can be used to refer to the same occurrence. Viewed from one angle they are temptations, from another they are tests or trials. The difference is in the motive of the one who initiates the trial or temptation. If it comes from the devil, it is a temptation. He intends for us to fail the test. If it is from God, it is a trial, and He wants us to be strengthened by it. He desires that we pass the test. Our father is like an assayer putting the ore to the test, allowing the furnace of affliction to burn away the dross that the pure gold of one's character might be revealed.

Let's take a closer look at James 1:2-4. Vincent says that the word translated "all" in the phrase "count it all joy" means, "wholly . . . without admixture of sorrow." The word translated "temptations" in the KJV actually means "trials." Thus, verses two through four of James 1 could be translated, "My brethren, consider it an entirely joyous thing when you encounter various trials, knowing that the trying of your faith produces endurance. But let endurance complete its work, so that you may be fully developed, lacking in nothing."

Now, let's look at the word "into" from the request, "Lead us not into temptation." Alexander Maclaren explained it very well. He says it is used in the same way we use it when we speak of a guard leading an inmate into prison. Once he is inside, the iron bars will be closed behind him and every precaution will be taken to prevent his escape. When one has been led into prison, he is trapped, closed in, and escape from it is difficult if not impossible. The same is true of temptation. If you were led into it, you would find it nearly impossible to escape. To change the metaphor somewhat, we might compare it to being led through a swamp by the unerring hand of our Guide. On every side are bogs we could fall into which would capture us in their mire. We pray that the Lord will not lead us into those places, that He won't allow us to be caught in the mire and held fast by evil. We don't want the prison doors to clang shut behind us leaving us no way of escape. We want Him to lead us not *into*, but *through* temptation to the place of safety and rest on the other side.

I Corinthians 10:13 tells us that He will do just that. "God is faithful, who will not allow you to be tempted beyond what you are able, but with the temptation will also make the way of escape, that you may be able to bear it."

If one has the right attitude toward temptations and if he faces them with faith and prayer, they will help him grow into a stronger and better servant of the Lord. That's what God intends when He allows us to be afflicted. He means it for our benefit. So, when we pray, "Lead us not into temptations," we are not asking to be spared from all trials and afflictions, but we are asking Him to so lead us that Satan will have no means of snaring us and dragging us down into the practice of sin. It should be a foregone conclusion that when we pray that prayer, we intend to do everything we can do to avoid those snares. We will not just float along with the tide in life, going wherever it takes us. We will co-operate with the Lord in building defenses against the attacks of Satan. In order to do that, we need to understand the process by which the devil tempts us to sin. Armed with that understanding, we can begin to build our defenses. The Bible describes for us the way the devil works, so we have only to study what it says to gain the understanding we seek. We will get to the scriptures in just a moment, but first let me point out one thing. We encounter circumstances every day which give the devil opportunities to tempt us. Of course, the Lord also uses those circumstances to test us, to burn away the dross and bring out the gold in our character. We are the ones who make the difference according to how we respond. Our responses to circumstances depend on what we love. The circumstances are outside of us. The devil must have something inside us to which he can make his appeal.

Let's look at two passages of scripture which, when taken together, show how Satan uses what we love to drag us down into sin. The first is James 1:13-15.

> Let no man say when he is tempted, I am tempted of God: for God cannot be tempted with evil, neither tempteth he any man: But every man is tempted, when he is drawn away of his own lust and enticed. Then when lust hath conceived, it bringeth forth sin: and sin, when it is finished bringeth forth death.

According to Vincent, the words translated "drawn away" and "enticed" in this passage are metaphors taken from hunting and fishing. The first refers to drawing an animal away from safe cover into an area full of traps and snares. The second is used to refer to enticing a fish with an attractive bait. The word "lust" in this passage (v. 15) is preceded by an article which indicates that it is a man's own personal desire which gives the devil an attractive bait to use to entice him. That desire may be a longing for wealth or prestige or power or fame. It may be a physical longing, for food or rest or sex, or it could be a desire for companionship. It isn't necessarily a bad desire, but it becomes bad if it is so strong that Satan can use it to lure us into sinful activities in our attempt to satisfy it. When we reach out to take the bait, that is, to satisfy our longing, Satan sets the hook and draws us away into sin.

The second passage is I John 2:15-16.

> Love not the world, neither the things that are in the world. If any man love the world, the love of the father is not in him. For all that is in the world, the lust of the flesh, the lust of the eyes, and the pride of life, is not of the father, but is of the world.

Notice the correlation between the words "love" and "lust." John indicated that loving the world involves desiring to give pleasure to the flesh, desiring to acquire the things the eyes covet, and desiring to elevate oneself above his fellows. To love the world is to lust after the things of the world. These are the lusts to which James was referring. If we love the world, if we set our hearts on its pleasures and possessions, Satan will have something he can use to set his hook and draw us away into sin.

Let's examine these ideas a little further. The lust of the flesh refers to those desires which arise because we live in bodies of flesh. It is natural for our flesh to desire certain things: food, water, rest, sex. But man does not live by bread alone. Our lives are not to be taken up with the flesh. We are not to set our hearts on the gratifying of those desires as if that were the meaning of life. To think of those things as more important than they really are gives the devil something into which he can sink his hook.

The lust of the eyes is the desire for things we can see, possessions. We are not to set our hearts on the acquisition of possessions. We are to treasure what is in heaven, to focus our affections on things above. The love of things which money can buy makes us susceptible, gives the devil a foothold, something he can use to tempt us.

The pride of life is the desire for recognition, for the acclaim of the world. It is the desire to be somebody special. We are not to cherish that desire, for if we do, it will give the devil an advantage he can use to drag us into sin.

What we learn from James 1:13-15 and I John 2:15-16 is that it is extremely important to love the Lord and the things of heaven rather than the world and everything in it. We must be careful about what we love. If we love the wrong things, it gives Satan all the advantage he needs to entice us to sin. That's what Paul was referring to in I Timothy 6:10 when he wrote, "the love of money is a root of all kinds of evil." Here then is the process of temptation: The devil takes note of what we love, then he uses circumstances to appeal to our desires for the wrong things. If we love those things enough, we do the thing Satan suggests to acquire them, even if we know we shouldn't. Let me show you how the process works with some illustrations from the Bible and from life.

When Abram and his nephew, Lot, returned to the land of Canaan after a time spent in Egypt during a famine, their flocks and herds had increased so much that they could not remain together. The forage in any one location wasn't sufficient for all their livestock.

That was the situation. We don't know exactly what led each man to make the decision he made at the time, but we do know quite a bit about them and there are some hints in the text which enables us to make some pretty good guesses about their motives. Abram was the head of the clan, the tribe. He was the patriarch. As such he had the right to say what each of them were to do. Had he been a man who loved the pre-eminence, no doubt Satan would have used that to tempt him. He would have said, "Look, you're the boss. Lot has to do what you tell him to do. Besides, you're not getting any younger. In the plain of the Jordan you could settle down. You wouldn't have to do any more of this constant traveling. You could relax in your old age and enjoy life." But Abram didn't love the feeling of power one gets from being able to order others around. He didn't love luxury or ease. His first love was trying to be the man God wanted him to be. So, he did the unselfish thing. He let Lot take his choice of the land.

But Lot was a different story. He loved to pamper himself. His subsequent history makes that evident. He wanted to live in a house, get out of that tent with all that moving. He enjoyed his wine and the pleasure of entertaining in his home. When he saw how easy it would be to provide year round grazing for his flocks and herds in the plains of the Jordan, he did the selfish thing. He chose the richest area for himself. If his uncle Abram was fool enough to offer it, he wasn't going to turn it down. You see, the devil knew what he loved and he used it to bring about his ruin and disgrace. Because he loved the wrong things, he lost his possessions, his family and his reputation. Satan also knows what we love, so we must make sure we love God and His way rather than the world and the things it can offer.

When George Washington Carver moved to Tuskegee,

Alabama, to work with Booker T. Washington at Tuskegee Institute, he went because he loved his people and wanted to help them. He soon discovered that the cotton land in much of the South was being worn out by failure to rotate crops. He began teaching the people that they could get a better return on their investment with less damage to the soil by raising peanuts and sweet potatoes. Many of them took his advice. So many, in fact, that there was soon a surplus of those two crops. They were rotting in the fields. Dr. Carver explained that he then turned to God and asked, "What is the peanut, and why did You make it?" Having asked that question, he went to work experimenting. Eventually he made nearly 300 useful products from the peanut; everything from candy to pickles, shaving lotion to printer's ink, lard to linoleum, and even axle grease. Turning to the sweet potato, he made more than 100 products from it. In every case he gave away his knowledge, the processes by which those products were made. He received no personal gain from any of his discoveries. He did it all, single handedly creating a broad market for the peanut and the sweet potato, just to benefit his people.

At one time he was offered a salary of $100,000 by someone who wanted to lure him away from Tuskegee. He refused it because he really cared nothing about money. He believed God had led him to do his work for the benefit of others. He wore ragged, patched clothing and gave away much of his meager salary helping worthy boys. Satan could not tempt Dr. Carver with money or worldly acclaim because he loved the right things: His Father in heaven, and his brothers and sisters on earth.

Let me give you one other illustration of how Satan uses what we love to get his hook into us and drag us down into sin. The name Christopher means Christ-bearer. Christopher Columbus believed that his name was a clear indication that God had called him to a special mission: to carry the light of Christ into the darkness of undiscovered heathen lands (*The Light and the Glory*, Marshall and Manuel, p.31). It was almost a passion with him and it was the one thing that convinced Ferdinand and

Isabella, the devout Catholic monarchs of Spain, to finance his expedition. But Columbus had a great love for riches and worldly acclaim. It was his desire that they give him three things in return for his services: one tenth of any riches which might be found in lands he discovered, the unprecedented title, "Admiral of the Ocean Sea," and the positions of Viceroy and Governor of all discovered lands.

Satan used those desires to corrupt Columbus. It was 14 years from the time he first sighted land in the Western Hemisphere until he died. During that time he did very little to convert any of the native peoples to Christ. He was, however, the guiding light to an influx of Spanish marauders who slaughtered more than 90% of those people in their mad quest for gold. Out of a population of more than 300,000, only about 30,000 were left. The man who considered it his mission to bear the light of Christ to the heathens of undiscovered lands allowed his love for wealth and power and acclaim to give Satan the advantage from which he would drag the great discoverer down to the depths of bitterness and disgrace.

The importance of setting our hearts on God, of treasuring the things of heaven instead of those of earth cannot be overstated. We simply must cultivate a love of the right things if we want to defeat Satan. If we pray, "lead us not into temptation," we must allow the Lord to transform our hearts so that we will learn to love what He loves.

A passage of Scripture that spells out what we should do to cultivate that love is found in the first Psalm.

> Blessed is the man that walketh not in the counsel of the ungodly, nor standeth in the way of sinners, nor sitteth in the seat of the scornful. But his delight is in the law of the Lord; and in his law doth he meditate day and night.

The Hebrew word translated "blessed" in that Psalm means, literally, "O how happy," and the remainder of verses one and two gives the key to living a happy, fulfilled life, one which thwarts

Satan's attempts to drag us down. It first gives the negative aspect of that life.

The one who is blessed does not walk in the counsel of the ungodly. That is, he does not conduct his life in accordance with the wisdom of men who do not acknowledge God. The ungodly are those who refuse to take God into account as they determine their course in life. Their counsel is their advice, their wisdom, their value system. What is the philosophy of the ungodly? "You've only got one life, so you've got to grab for all the gusto you can." "Eat, drink and be merry, for tomorrow we die." What does the world value? Youth, beauty, intelligence, and money. If you don't have those things, you are worthless. That's the rationale for abortion and euthanasia. If it is unwanted, destroy it, get rid of it. The Bible answer: I John 2:17, "The world passeth away, and the lust thereof; but he that doeth the will of God abideth forever." None of the things the world values will last; not youth, or money, or intelligence, or beauty. One day all the "gusto" will be gone from each of our lives if we live long enough. The lust will pass away. Appetite and taste for food will fade, the desire for power and acclaim will give way to a desire to stop suffering, and possessions will be worthless when we stand on the brink of the grave. The only thing that will matter is the will of God. The world's philosophies and its values are foolish. Only he who rejects them and orders his life according to the will of God is truly happy.

Blessed is the man who does not stand in the way of sinners. He does not frequent those places where sinners congregate. He does not desire the friendship of the world. He is not interested in being one of the crowd. He desires acceptance among them only as one who cares about them and seeks to lead them to Christ. He does not try to be acceptable among them by imitating their clothing, their music or their attitudes. He isn't interested in sounding tough, or macho, or "with it." He knows that friendship with the world is enmity with Christ. He seeks to project an image of compassion, willingness to serve, humility and joyous living.

Blessed is the man who does not sit in the seat of the scornful. He is not at home with those who mock religion, no matter how highly acclaimed they may be. The most renowned scientists don't get his admiration if they reject his Lord. He does not read their books, see their movies or listen to their propaganda. They may be wealthy, sophisticated, idolized by the world, but if they show their ignorance of what is true and good by renouncing Christ, they don't appeal to him.

But even more important than the things the truly blessed man rejects and avoids are the things in which he delights. "His delight is in the law of the Lord; and in his law doth he meditate day and night." By spending much time in study and meditation on the words of the Lord, he comes to delight more and more in them. He sees the beauty of holiness, the loveliness of being good, and the great joy of righteous living.

The sophisticated, the tough, the macho may be glamorous, but there is certainly no real beauty or loveliness in them. It is in the gentle, compassionate, the humble, the brave, the generous, the unselfish, and in those who give freely of themselves for the benefit of others that you find the real loveliness in this world.

My brethren, let me urge you to spend time in reading and meditating on the word of God, on His wisdom and goodness. Spend time with the Lord in prayer. Those are the only ways I know of to cultivate a love for the right things, and that we must do if we hope to come out a winner in the battle with Satan. It is in doing those things that we allow the Lord to lead us through temptation rather than into it.

The teaching of the word of God is very clear. We are taught to pray, "Lead us not into temptation." In teaching us that, Jesus was showing us that we should be aware of our weaknesses. We should realize that Satan has great ability to entice us, and that our only hope for victory over him lies in our following the lead of our Savior. Our greatest desire in life should be the desire to live holy lives in imitation of our Master, and our greatest dread should be the possibility of falling into sin.

## Discussion Questions

1. How can you harmonize the two ideas expressed in Scripture, one which Jesus taught, "lead us not into temptation" and one which James taught, "count it all joy when ye fall into divers temptations"?

2. Why does God allow us to face trials and tribulations?

3. Explain how God can lead us while we are in the midst of temptations without leading us into them.

4. Why is it so important that we love the right things?

5. Explain what it means to you to "set your heart" on something.

6. Can you think of some people you know personally who just don't seem to care about money or the things money can buy? Are they that way because they care most deeply about the things of God and heaven?

7. How do people who have rejected the world's value system fit into American society? How do you think people would treat you if you showed by your actions that you did not value money, possessions, prestige, success, acclaim, luxury, personal beauty, education, and all the other things the world considers important?

8. How do you think a person comes to love the things of God rather than the things of the world?

9. God loved the world so much that He gave His Son to die that the world might be saved. Of course, the world He loved was not the material world, but the world of men. He loved

all the people of the human race. He also taught us to love our fellow men. What traits of character demonstrate that we love people as He loves them?

## Chapter Eleven
# DELIVER US FROM EVIL

"But deliver us from evil" is the positive aspect of the petition presented in the preceding clause, "Lead us not into temptation." The conjunction "but" makes it evident that we have here an opposing clause. The opposite of being led into temptation is being delivered from evil.

However, there is a broader application of this last petition of the Lord's Prayer. It is based on a fuller understanding of the biblical use of the term "evil." That word is sometimes used in the Bible to refer to anything which produces pain, sorrow, or suffering of any kind. Thus, we read that Job spoke of the great calamities which befell him as evil. When Satan had taken away all of Job's wealth, had brought about the death of all of his children, and had stricken him with boils from his head to his feet, the patriarch's wife said to him, "Dost thou still retain thine integrity? Curse God and die." Job's reply to that advice was magnificent, "Thou speaketh as one of the foolish women speaketh. What? shall we receive good at the hand of God, and shall we not receive evil?" (Job 2:9,10). You see, Job called his suffering evil.

Jesus used the word "evil" in the same way. In Matthew 6:34 He said, "Take therefore no thought for the morrow: for the morrow shall take thought for the things of itself. Sufficient unto the day is the evil thereof." Modern translators have paraphrased that last sentence thus: "every day has enough trouble of its own." So, you see, the troubles we endure are called "evil" in the Bible.

When we use this broader sense of the word "evil" in our petition, "deliver us from evil," it becomes a very comprehensive request and an expression of the bright hope we have in Jesus. We look forward to a day when all that brings us pain: all sin, all disgrace, all suffering, and dying will come to an end, and we will serve our Lord night and day in His temple with gladness. But today, right now, we seek deliverance from those forces which bring us hunger or disease or pain of any kind. We seek deliverance from the evil within us and deliverance from the clutches of Satan.

## *DELIVERANCE FROM SUFFERING*

Let's consider first the cry for deliverance from the evil of suffering. Notice that it is not a plea for exemption from suffering, but deliverance from it. We are not asking to be spared from the universal experience of all mankind. When Adam and Eve sinned in the Garden of Eden, they brought down the curse upon the human race, and every person who has lived from that day to this one has experienced pain, sorrow, and suffering. We are not asking Him to make us exempt from that. We are not saying, "Spare us from suffering." We are saying, "Deliver us."

There are various ways in which He does that. One of those ways is by showing us how to bear it and how to gain from it. The scriptures teach that it is God's intention to use suffering to mold us into the people He wants us to be. Joni Eareckson says that if she had not experienced that accident which paralyzed her from the shoulders down, she never would have developed the relationship with the Lord which she enjoys today; in fact, she says she may not have been faithful to Him at all.

We know the Lord allows us to suffer in order to shape our character in the image of Jesus Christ. We know it from our own personal experience. Several years ago my dear wife, Diane, went through an extended period of rather deep depression. She and I together talked and prayed and read and (by the grace of God) worked our way through that time. Because of that experience, we are both much stronger in the faith. For several years now she has had the privilege of counseling with different ladies who have been fighting depression. She is able to bless their lives, to be a real help to them, because of what God allowed her to suffer. She has even conducted several seminars on "How to deal with depression." That's the way God intends for suffering to affect us. He wants it to make us stronger and better, more full of faith, and better able to serve the needs of others. In the depth of the distress that suffering brings we learn to rely on God more completely than we ever would if we only experienced prosperity. In the face of difficulty, we learn how weak we are and how very much we need Him.

Of course, that is not the only way He delivers us from the evil of suffering. Sometimes He takes the pain away. We have prayed many times for people who were suffering terribly, and we have seen God make them well. It has happened over and over again and we praise God for His tender compassion. We bless His holy name because He is so good, so merciful and kind. Those answers to prayer also increase our faith.

Now, notice that He taught us to pray not only for our own personal deliverance, but for the deliverance of others as well.

Have you seen the fact that every one of the petitions of the Lord's Prayer which have to do with the needs of men contain the word "us"? "Give *us* this day our daily bread, forgive *us* our debts as we forgive our debtors. Lead *us* not into temptation, but deliver *us* from evil." He teaches us not to be selfish, to care as much about deliverance from evil for our brothers and sisters as we care about it for ourselves. We ought to be praying for the Christian family all over the world.

There was a time when Peter was concerned about what reward he and the other apostles would receive for having forsaken all to follow Jesus. The Lord responded to him by saying, "Verily, I say unto you, there is no man that hath left houses, or brethren, or sisters, or father, or mother, or wife, or children, or lands, for my sake, and the gospel's, but he shall receive an hundred fold now in this time, houses, and brethren, and sisters, and mothers, and children, and lands, with persecutions; and in the world to come eternal life" (Mark 10:29,30).

Do you see what He meant? I've got a brother in Kansas City, a brother in Alaska, and a sister in Memphis, Tennessee. I don't get to see them very often. I've only seen my brother in Alaska once in the past ten years. I've left home and parents, and brothers and a sister to preach the gospel; but I've got brothers and sisters right here where I am who are just as dear to me as my own flesh and blood brothers. The Lord has given me far more than a hundred fold for all I left behind.

We are truly brothers and sisters. If we love each other as we are supposed to, we will care as much about our family in the Lord as we do about ourselves. We will want all of them to be delivered from evil just as surely as we want deliverance for ourselves. I tell you frankly, I have received phone calls about brothers and sisters in Christ which told us that they had cancer, and it hurt deeply. There are very few things in this life more devastating than the hearing of those words, "It's malignant." It hurts when those we love receive that verdict. We ought to be as concerned about their deliverance from the evil of cancer as we would be if the doctor had told us we had the disease.

It may be that none of us are hungry, but we've got brothers and sisters in India and Africa and Haiti and other places who are starving. We must cry out to God for their deliverance as well as for our own. Then we must do everything God has given us the ability to do to lift their burden and share with them in their need.

We are free, but we have brothers and sisters in Communist lands who are living in virtual slavery. It behoves us, if we care as the Lord taught us to care, to pray that they might be delivered from the horrors of that totalitarian system. Just a while back I read about two newsmen who were discussing the experience of walking down a street of a large city in a Communist country. They were each thinking there was something about it that was quite different from walking the sidewalks of any city in the West. Suddenly it dawned on one of them. He said, "The only thing we heard there was the tramp, tramp of people's feet. There was no exchange of pleasant greetings. Most everyone just looked down at the ground as they trudged along in their misery." We have brothers and sisters who are enduring that day after day, year after year. We must pray, "O God, deliver them from that terrible evil." Beyond praying for them, we can contribute to organizations which take Bibles and other Christian literature to our brothers and sisters behind the iron curtain. T.C.M. International, Inc. (6337 Hollister Dr., Indianapolis, IN, 46224) is one such organization. They take our love and encouragement as they go. We need to support that work and pray for them. I tell you sincerely, I would be ashamed to write these words if I worshipped in air conditioned church buildings with padded pews and wore good clothing and had more than enough to eat if I were not giving something regularly to help meet the needs of brothers and sisters in other parts of the world. If we are going to ask God to deliver our brethren from evil, we had better make sure our lives are consistent with that prayer.

I believe we should pray for this world, that God would deliver it from the great evils that plague it. "Deliver us from war and pestilence, from famine, terrorism, and Communism." I believe it is appropriate for us to pray that our world might be delivered from the awful diseases that claim so many lives and devastate so many families. Let's pray that God might lead the researchers to find a cure for cancer and heart disease and all the things that bring suffering, pain, and heartaches in our world.

## *DELIVERANCE FROM EVIL INFLUENCE*

Consider then the cry for deliverance from those forces of evil which attempt to turn us against God and moral uprightness. It is difficult for Christian people to imagine that there are those in our society who not only approve of abortion, pornography, prostitution, the liquor and drug traffic, and homosexuality, but who actively promote those evils.

Take a look at what Dr. James Dobson wrote in a letter to Focus on the Family supporters in May, 1988, about this very thing: "I could fill several books with my great concern for this country and the moral disintegration that seems to be occurring. Suddenly, now, the very foundation appears to be giving way. Many signs point to the unraveling of a value system that has served us so well since the Pilgrims landed at Plymouth Rock in 1620.

"These disturbing developments are not merely a function of their own internal momentum. They are being orchestrated with great care by those who hate the Christian system of values and are passionately dedicated to its destruction. A formidable army has been assembled on the battlefield, including the gay and lesbian movement; the National Organization for Women and all its minions; the American Civil Liberties Union; People for the American Way; the Mafia and the street-corner pushers who are destroying our kids with drugs; the medical personnel who are slaughtering our unborn babies; the euthanasia organizations that are urging us to kill the old, the sick and the handicapped; the

Planned Parenthood types who want to distribute condoms and amoral advice to American teenagers; the creators of sexploitation movies and terrible television programs that are seducing our kids and contributing to the spread of sexually transmitted diseases; the pornographers who are polluting our landscape; the self-consumed politicians who are taxing the family into oblivion; the early childhood educators and legislators who intend to socialize the raising of children in America; and, of course, the media, the universities and the judiciary, which are overwhelmingly committed to the humanistic perspective. These are the shock troops arrayed in full battle gear before us."

To those of us who love the Lord and see the winsome beauty of His law and His way, it seems incredible that there could be so many powerful people who hate that way so thoroughly. It has now, however, become imperative that we open our eyes to the fact that the forces of evil are succeeding in their quest to turn America into a Pagan society. Let me give a couple of illustrations to prove my point.

In one generation the sexual revolution has swept across this great nation turning the hearts of the American people to unbridled sexual passion. The beginning point for the hedonistic philosophy was the acceptance of the theory of evolution. When one has accepted the idea that he is an animal and differs from other animals only in complexity, morality goes out the window. That very fact is the number one reason the advocates of evolution have pushed Darwin's ideas so relentlessly. Erwin Lutzer in *The Rebirth of America* says, "On a television program, author Aldous Huxley once responded to a question of why evolution was so readily accepted. He admitted,'the reason we accepted Darwinism even without proof is because we didn't want God to interfere with our sexual mores.' " When society at large had accepted evolution, the next step was easy.

In 1954 Hugh Hefner opened the floodgates of filth with the first issue of *Playboy*. In cleverly planned articles it attacked Judeo-Christian morality. Within a few years he had built a $170 million empire on that theme. The depth of his depravity has been documented by Dr. Judith A. Reisman in a study she did for the United States Department of Justice. She examined every issue of *Playboy, Penthouse,* and *Hustler* magazines which had been published at the time of her study. She discovered that children were depicted in those magazines an average of about 9 times per issue — from the very beginning. The depictions were such that it can be said truthfully that those magazines have been encouraging child molestation and sex with children for all those years. Perhaps the most frightening thing about these things is that the national media and government have acted in such a way as to make them acceptable. The national television networks treat their publishers as respected businessmen and Congress has appropriated money to publish them in braille.

Another front in the battle to destroy the influence of Christianity in America is the public school classroom. In the May-June, 1987, issue of *Exposing Satan's Power*, Ben Alexander explained that "19th century Humanist Wilhelm Von Humboldt wrote, 'Whatever we wish to see introduced into a life or a nation must first be introduced into its schools.'

"This quote from *The Humanist* magazine, dated January/February 1983 entitled 'A Religion For A New Age,' declares the strategy that the Humanists have chosen. 'I am convinced that the battle for humankind's future must be waged and won in the public school classroom by teachers who correctly preceive their role as the proselytizers of a new faith. These teachers must embody the same selfless dedication as the most rabid fundamentalist preachers, for they will be ministers of another sort, utilizing a classroom instead of a pulpit to convey humanist values in whatever subjects they teach, regardless of the educational level — preschool, daycare or large state university.

" 'The classroom must and will become an arena of conflict between the old and the new — the rotting corpse of Christianity, together with all its adjacent evils and misery, and the new faith of Humanism, resplendent in its promise of a world in which the never realized Christian ideal of "love thy neighbor" will finally be achieved.' "

It should be evident from that quote that there are people who hate Christianity. Can you believe he would speak of it as "the rotting corpse of Christianity, together with all its adjacent evils?" If you want to see how the Humanists are working toward their goals in the public schools, read *Child Abuse in the Classroom*, by Phyllis Schlafly and *What Are They Teaching Our Children*, by Mel and Norma Gabler.

I could give you many additional facts about those who are actively promoting evil in America today, but my purpose here is only to illustrate that fact. I want to encourage you to pray, "O God, please deliver us from the forces of evil that would turn us away from goodness and from You." We also need to be informed about the growing influence of Islam, Hinduism, other Eastern religions, the occult, and secular humanism in our judicial and legislative branches of government. We need to pray, "Father, deliver us from those evils. Give us the courage we need to take a firm stand against them."

## *DELIVERANCE FROM THE EVIL WITHIN*

Then I would have you consider the cry for deliverance from the evil within us. Perhaps it is the greatest evil of all. I mean the evil that would lead us to think always of self and not of others, the evil that would hold a grudge, the vindictive spirit; "deliver us from those evils."

Deliverance from sin and its consequences comes through God's forgiveness. The only way to escape paying the penalty for sin is by receiving the forgiveness of God in the way He tells us about in the Bible. The only way to be delivered from the bondage of sin, that enslavement which makes us the servants of our lower impulses, is through the presence of the Holy Spirit in our lives. It is the Holy Spirit who comes into our hearts and takes out the vindictiveness and replaces it with mercy and compassion and love for others. It is the Holy Spirit of God who teaches us to love not the things of this world, but to love God and His way, to love God and goodness.

The Lord made a promise to us through the Apostle Peter. On the day the church was born He promised that all those who would repent and be baptized would receive the remission of their sins and the indwelling presence of the Holy Spirit. Further, he said that the promise would be for all those who heard along with their childen and "all who are afar off" (Acts 2:38,39). In other words, the promise is for us and all who obey Him from a sincere heart.

A further promise is found in Luke 11:9-13:

> And I say to you, ask, and it will be given to you; seek, and you will find; knock, and it will be opened to you. For everyone who asks receives, and he who seeks finds, and to him who knocks it will be opened. If a son asks for bread from any father among you, will he give him a stone? If you then, being evil, know how to give good gifts to your children, how much more will your heavenly Father give the Holy Spirit to those who ask Him?

The more we want the influence of the Holy Spirit in our lives, and the more we ask for His presence, the more we will be able to defeat Satan. He delivers us from the evil within us by giving us His Holy Spirit. We need to pray, "Deliver us, O God, from the evil within us, by filling us with Your Spirit."

I think, perhaps, the greatest teaching of this portion of the Lord's Prayer is the idea that we are totally dependent upon God for our deliverance. There are forces of evil which would surely overcome us except for the fact that the one who is in us is greater than he that is in the world. We will win the victory through Jesus Christ. Thank God, there will come a day when all the evil will be behind us. All sin and suffering and dying will be past. All our failures to live up to what we ought to be will be over. We shall be like Him for we shall see Him as He is. We will be with Him, and there will be joy in the presence of the Lord forever.

## Discussion Questions

1. What are some of the ways God grants deliverance from the evil of suffering? Explain the difference between exemption from pain and suffering and deliverance from them.

2. Can you tell of a time when God allowed you to suffer in order to prepare you to help others who are facing similar experience?

3. Can you tell of a personal experience when the Lord healed you or a loved one?

4. What obligations come to us when we pray for our brothers and sisters in foreign lands to be delivered from the evils their poverty brings upon them?

5. When we pray for deliverance from the evil forces that seek to destroy what morality there is left in our society, what obligations come to us? What must we do to oppose those forces of evil?

6. What are some of the evil tendencies within us from which we should seek deliverance?

7. In Romans 12:2 Paul admonishes us to be "transformed by the renewing of (our) minds." How do you think one renews his mind? Does that renewing of the mind strengthen one against the forces of evil against which we struggle?

## Chapter Twelve
# THE DOXOLOGY

The Lord's Prayer closes with a doxology which is a short ascription of praise. The words, "For thine is the kingdom, and the power, and the glory, forever Amen." are not found in some of the ancient manuscripts. There are those who conclude, therefore, that they should not be in our Bibles. I am not among them. But whatever you may conclude in regard to that, the truth remains that most everyone agrees that they are perfectly appropriate as a close for the model prayer. That is enough to convince me that they were spoken by our Lord. Who else could have devised a perfect doxology for the end of a perfect prayer?

We might well ask, "Why would Jesus teach His followers to bring their prayers to a close with praise?" I think the answer may be seen in the use of the word "for" at the beginning of the doxology. It indicates that that which follows gives the rationale for presenting the petitions of this prayer to our Lord. It makes sense to ask the One who has all power for our daily supply of bread. It is rational to seek forgiveness from the One to whom all authority belongs. It is logical to desire that the name of the all glorious One may be held in highest reverence by all men.

As we praise Him, we remind ourselves of His dominion, His power, and His glory. Thus we enhance our confidence in His ability and His willingness to answer our prayers. Praise is a faith strengthening exercise. Jesus taught us to praise the Father because He knew that the more we meditate upon His greatness, the more we will be able to trust Him.

## *HOW TO PRAISE*

Jesus taught us the proper way to praise the Father with this doxology. It is a bit surprising that we should need such instruction. We know how to praise our spouses and our children. When my daughters come home from school with high marks on their report cards, I say, "I'm so proud of you!" When they do something kind and generous for their mother or a neighbor, I say, "You are good daughters, and I'm proud to be your daddy." Can you guess how they respond to that kind of praise? Sometimes they say, "You're a good daddy, and we love you." I know how to praise my wife. I believe she makes the world's finest biscuits. Nobody can make them better. Not too long ago she made some that were even better than usual. They may have been the best biscuits ever made. I told her she was the best biscuit maker in the world. That got a nice smile from her and a sweet "Thank you." Then she threw in a few hugs and kisses just to let me know how much she appreciated that praise.

Why should we need to be taught how to praise God when we know how to praise others? Maybe because we've never really done it. It seems strange to many people to say to God, "I think

You are the greatest. There is no One like You! You are more kind and generous and loving and merciful than I ever dreamed anyone could be. It just seems incredible that One so powerful, so holy, so wise as You are could want me to be Your son. It is a wonderful joy to me to be called Your child."

When one of my daughters tells me I'm a good daddy, it gives me great joy. I want to be, and if she thinks I am, well, there's just no other feeling quite like that. I want to give that same kind of joy to my heavenly Father. I want to say to Him that I think He is the greatest Father, that He is far greater than I can even imagine. He knows that the more I realize how great He is the more I'll be able to trust Him, and the more I'll become the kind of son He wants me to be.

## *THINE IS THE KINGDOM*

The first statement of praise Jesus taught us in the doxology was, "Thine is the kingdom." That is to say that the kingdom belongs to Him. It is His by right. He is the king. He has the right to rule, to universal dominion.

He rules the physical universe. All nature moves at His command. The sun, the moon, the stars, and the planets continue in their appointed courses, performing the tasks He assigned to them because it is His will. The sun shines, the rain falls, the crops grow as He sees fit. When we recognize that, we will feel confident to ask Him to provide our bread each day. We know He can do it.

Of course, bread is not our only physical need. I'm thinking about illness and our need for deliverance from it. One of the most interesting stories in the gospels is found in Luke 7:1-10. It is the story of a Roman centurion who came to Jesus asking that a beloved servant be healed. He sent a message to the Lord saying, "Trouble not thyself: for I am not worthy that thou shouldest enter under my roof . . . but say in a word, and my servant shall be healed" (vv. 6,7). He recognized that Jesus had authority over all nature and he knew it wasn't necessary for Him to be present to heal his servant. It is as we recognize that authority that we find it appropriate to go to Him for the healing of our infirmities.

He also has the right to rule in the affairs of men and nations. We Christians recognize that fact. We have chosen Him as our King and we are His loyal subjects. We look to Him for guidance so that we may order our affairs to please Him. We want our jobs, our families, our leisure time, our education, our worship, in short, everything in our lives to conform to His will. We seek through study and prayer to know that will, and we determine through self-discipline and the assistance of the Holy Spirit to do it. But what about men and nations who do not submit to His will? Does He rule in their affairs as well? He does! Pharaoh found that out when He tried to resist the will of God. When ten plagues had been visited upon Egypt, he finally released the Israelites. Perhaps even more significantly, God used a pagan nation, Babylon under Nebuchadnezzar, to punish and purify His people in Judah. Habakkuk was deeply concerned about how God could do that. How could He use a nation of idolaters, more wicked than Judah, to punish His people? The answer to the prophet's question is found in chapter two of his book. God says that Babylon is but an instrument through which His righteous judgment will be brought upon Judah, and Babylon in its arrogance will also feel His wrath when the time is right.

An illustration of the way God overrules the plans of men may be seen in the story Jesus told of the rich fool (Luke 12:16-21). The man's ground produced a bountiful harvest, so much that he didn't have room to store it all. So he made plans to tear down his old barns and build bigger ones, to store up all his goods and retire to a life of ease. He planned to eat, drink, and be merry for many years; but God said to him, "Thou fool, this night thy soul shall be required of thee." But God uses ordinary events in our lives more than extraordinary intervention to direct the courses we will take. For Enoch it seems to have been the birth of his first child that brought about a change in his life. Perhaps it was the responsibility of fatherhood that made him think seriously about life. At any rate, from that day forward he walked with God (Gen. 5:21-24). For Peter it was his failure on the night Jesus was arrested. He denied even knowing the Lord three times. From that day on he was a changed man. He was no longer the blustering, self-assured, impulsive Simon. He became Peter, the rock, grounded in Jesus; finding his strength and assurance in the Lord. For Paul, there was always the memory of the day he officiated at the stoning of Stephen. He could never forget how he had persecuted the church, and he could never work hard enough for Jesus to erase that memory from his mind. He would always consider himself the "chief of sinners" and an unprofitable servant. Just so, God uses the ordinary events of men's lives to bring about His will. Even if they don't surrender those lives to Him, He can so order events that His will may be accomplished.

Knowing that our God does rule in the affairs of men and nations enables us to pray with confidence, "Deliver us from evil." We can confidently seek deliverance from the evils of Communism and terrorism, from corrupt politicians who would destroy America, and from a court system which allows gambling, prostitution, abortion and pornography, and outlaws Bible reading and prayer and the teaching of creation science in our public schools.

When we pray, "Thine is the kingdom," we recognize our Father's right to the allegiance of all men. We pray, "Thy kingdom come," because we desire that all men own Him as their King and give Him their loyal allegiance. We pray, "Thy will be done in earth as it is in heaven," because giving that allegiance will mean surrendering themselves to Him as clay in the potter's hands to be shaped according to His will.

He also has the right to rule over the spiritual realm. That means all spiritual beings must obey His will. Angels and even demons must obey Him. The demons seek, in their allegiance to Satan, to thwart His will; but when He gives them a direct command, they have no choice, they must obey.

Since He does rule the spiritual realm, He has the right to demand justice or to extend mercy. Forgiveness, or pardon must come from Him. He alone has the right to give it. He alone has the right to set down the conditions on which pardon will be granted. He has established those conditions and they are spelled out rather plainly in the New Testament. To receive forgiveness from God one must believe (John 3:16). Hebrews 11:6 tells us it is impossible to please Him without faith. That faith includes belief in His existence and trust in His promises. To receive forgiveness one must repent and be baptized. Acts 2:38 indicates that we do those two things in order to acquire remission of sins and the gift of the Holy Spirit. To repent is to make up your mind to turn away from sin and to surrender your will to God. Baptism is immersion in water in the name of the Father, the Son, and the Holy Spirit (Matt. 28:18-20). Faith is not a meritorious act by which one earns salvation. Neither is repentance or baptism. To earn anything one must perform some service roughly equal in worth to the pay received. Faith, repentance, and baptism have no significant value as meritorious works. As works they cannot be compared with feeding the hungry, sheltering the homeless, or witnessing to the lost. The one who reaches out to God in faith by making up his mind to turn away from sin and by allowing himself to be baptized has simply fulfilled the provisions God has established for accepting the pardon He offers.

When we pray, "Thine is the kingdom," we should give ourselves time to contemplate all that means. Our meditation will then be praise to Him who holds dominion over all.

Don DeWelt suggests that we should write out our prayers or say them out loud. He teaches that these are two effective ways for assuring ourselves that we will concentrate on what we are doing and keep our minds from wandering. But our minds will always be able to move much more rapidly than our hands can write or our mouths can speak, so there is still room for wandering.

My suggestion would be that we make brief notes as we pray, and then allow our minds to explore all the possibilities connected with those notes. We might write, for example, "Thine is the kingdom," and under that write, "rule," "men and nations," "physical universe," and "spiritual realm." Those notes will remind us of the specifics of His universal dominion. We will praise Him in our hearts for His wisdom in guiding the affairs of men and nations, for His generosity in providing for our physical needs, and for His mercy in granting us forgiveness.

## *THINE IS THE POWER*

In the second place, Jesus taught us to pray, "Thine is the power." There is some overlapping here with the first category of praise. The right to rule must be augmented by the power to rule. Some of the answers we receive to our prayers depend on that power as well as on His authority.

When we pray, "Thine is the power," we are saying that all power resides in Him, exists through Him, and has its source in Him. All power includes the power to create, the power to sustain creation, and the power to give or deny life to His creatures. When we praise Him with these words, we acknowledge that power. He created the heavens and the earth and all that is in them.

When I think of the creation power of God, I think not only of the physical heavens and earth. I think of the human mind and all its capabilities. The ability to remember, to dream, to design, to invent, to make music, to love, to honor, to worship — all were made by God when He made the mind of man.

Music is an interesting creation. Do you realize that it exists only as a function of memory? We can only hear one note at a time. The melody we "hear" is actually a combination of the one note we are hearing and those which have come before it — along with our anticipation of the ones to come.

Language is another function of memory. We must remember the meaning of words. We must also remember what has been said, because we can only hear one word at a time. To communicate a complex message or to learn a new skill involves an incredible capability to remember.

Let me illustrate: To drive my car I must remember that it takes a key to start it and that only one key will fit the ignition lock. I must remember to turn it to the right until the engine starts, at which time I must release the key. I must remember to use my right foot at the same time to push down on the accelerator — not too much. The list is endless, yet driving is a relatively simple skill. We don't even consciously think of most of those things when we do them. But if you have ever designed anything, you know that you must think of every detail or your product will be incomplete. Just so, God had to think of endless details to make the human mind the complete marvel it is. When I meditate on these things it makes me want to cry out, "O Lord, my God how great thou art!"

You could also spend a good deal of time just contemplating the sustaining power of God, and His power to give life. Two verses of scripture speak clearly of His sustaining power: Colossians 1:17 and Hebrews 1:3. The former says that by Him all things "hold together," and the latter says He upholds "all things by the word of his power." Think of everything "holding together" in the light of the modern scientific discovery that every particle of matter is made up of atoms which are held together by some mysterious force, a force so powerful that splitting of atoms results in explosions more powerful than any man had ever produced. How great is the power of God which holds all things together?

Consider the life-giving power of God. Again, realize that life as we know it was God's idea; plant life; animal life; consciousness and self-consciousness. Animals have conscious life, but they don't know it. Only man has the ability to say, "I exist," and "I know I exist." Pseudo scientists may claim that life began spontaneously, the chance combination of chemicals, but only one who has not examined all the evidence or one who has predetermined that supernatural is unfeasable would believe such nonsense.

It is our acceptance of the fact that all power resides in Him that gives us the confidence to ask Him to "Lead us not into temptation, but deliver us from evil." His ability to answer those prayers depends on what we call "providential" power. It includes His perfect wisdom and His ability to alter everyday matters in such a way as to change our course of action at a given time. The following story is a wonderful illustration of God's providence.

## *WHY THE CHOIR WAS LATE*

"It happened on the evening of March 1 in the town of Beatrice, Neb. In the afternoon the Reverend Walter Klempel had gone to the West Side Baptist Church to get things ready for choir practice. He lit the furnace — most of the singers were in the habit of arriving around 7:15, and it was chilly in the church — and went home to dinner. But at 7:10, when it was time for him to go back to the church with his wife and daughter, Marilyn Ruth, it turned out that Marilyn Ruth's dress was soiled, so Mrs. Klempel ironed another. Thus they were still at home when it happened.

"Ladona Vandegrift, a high school sophomore, was having trouble with a geometry problem. She knew practice began promptly and always came early. But she stayed to finish the problem.

"Royena Estes was ready, but the car would not start. So she and her sister, Sadie, called Ladona Vandegrift, and asked her to pick them up. But Ladona was the girl with the geometry problem, and the Estes sisters had to wait.

"Mrs. Leonard Schuster would ordinarily have arrived at 7:20 with her small daughter, Susan. But on this particular evening she had to go to her mother's house to help her get ready for a missionary meeting.

"Herbert Kipf, lathe operator, would have been ahead of time but had put off an important letter. 'I can't think why,' he said. He lingered over it and was late.

"It was a cold evening. Stenographer Joyce Black, feeling 'just plain lazy,' stayed in her warm house until the last possible moment. She was almost ready to leave.

"Because his wife was away, machinist Harvey Ahl was taking care of his two boys. He was going to take them to practice with him, but somehow he got wound up talking. When he looked at his watch, he saw he was already late.

"Marilyn Paul, the pianist, had planned to arrive half an hour early. However, she fell asleep after dinner, and when her mother awakened her at 7:15 she had time only to tidy up and start out.

"Mrs. F.E. Paul, choir director, and mother of the pianist, was late simply because her daughter was. She had tried unsuccessfully to awaken the girl earlier.

"High school girls Lucille Jones and Dorothy Wood are neighbors and customarily go to practice together. Lucille was listening to a 7 to 7:30 radio program and broke her habit of promptness because she wanted to hear the end. Dorothy waited for her.

"At 7:25, with a roar heard in almost every corner of Beatrice, the West Side Baptist Church blew up. The walls fell outward, the heavy wooden roof crashed straight down like the weight in a deadfall. But, because of such matters as a soiled dress, a cat nap, an unfinished letter, a geometry problem, and a stalled car, all of the members of the choir were late — something which had never occurred before.

"Firemen thought the explosion had been caused by natural gas, which may have leaked into the church from a broken pipe outside and had been ignited by the fire in the furnace. The Beatrice choir members had no particular theory about the fire's cause, but each of them began to reflect on the heretofore inconsequential details of his life, wondering at exactly what point it is that one can say, 'This is an act of God' " (From *The 30th Anniversay Reader's Digest Reader*, pp. 250-1).

My favorite story about how God works in behalf of His children is about a man born in Hungary. His name was Bela Paskin. On January 10, 1948, another Hungarian-American named Marcel Sternberger boarded a subway in New York City. He had been to visit a sick friend, and was riding this particular line for the first time in his life. As he boarded the subway car, a man sitting close to the door got up to leave and Sternberger slipped into the vacated seat — the only one available. Then he noticed that the man in the next seat was reading a Hungarian language newspaper. Under ordinary circumstances he wouldn't have spoken to the other passengers, but something seemed to prompt him to say in Hungarian, "I hope you don't mind if I glance at your paper." It was the beginning of a conversation which had amazing results.

The man was Bela Paskin. He had been a student before World War II, but was pressed into military service. When the war was over, he covered hundreds of miles on foot to return to his home town, Debrecen, a large city in eastern Hungary. Mr. Sternberger was familiar with the city. They talked about where Paskin had lived, and the fact that he had come home to discover that his entire family had been taken away by the Nazis to Auschwitz. When Paskin thought of the gas chambers, he gave up all hope of their having survived. A few days later he set out on foot to leave Hungary. He stole across border after border until he reached Paris. From there he managed to emigrate to the United States in October, 1947, just three months before he met Sternberger on the subway.

While they talked, Sternberger kept thinking that something seemed familiar about the story he was hearing. Suddenly he knew why. He had recently met a young woman from Debrecen at the home of friends. She had been sent to Auschwitz. Later she was liberated by the Americans and was brought to the U.S. in the first boatload of Displaced Persons in 1946. He had written down her address and phone number because she seemed so alone. He hoped his family could do something to help fill the emptiness for her.

After asking Bela a few leading questions, Sternberger said, "Let's get off the train." He led Paskin to a phone booth, found the number in his address book, and dialed it. In a few moments he had Marya Paskin on the line. He asked her where she had lived in Debrecen, and she told him the address. Asking her to hold the line, he turned to Bela and said, "Did your wife live on such-and-such street?" "Yes!" he exclaimed. He was white as a sheet and trembling. "Try to be calm," said Sternberger. "Something miraculous is about to happen to you. Here, take this telephone and talk to your wife!"

Bela nodded, bewildered, his eyes bright with tears. He took the receiver, listened a moment, then suddenly cried, "This is Bela! This is Bela!" He was so hysterical that Sternberger had to take the phone back. He calmed Marya the best he could and told her to stay where she was, he was sending her husband to her.

There were simply too many things which fell into place for that reunion to have occurred by coincidence. Mr. Sternberger had never ridden that particular subway line before. He never spoke to other passengers. There was only one seat available — the one next to Bela. His meeting with Mrs. Paskin had occurred so recently that he was able to remember the details of their conversation. He had written down her address and phone number because he felt compassion for her. The only logical conclusion is that God was riding the subway in New York that day (From *The Reader's Digest 40th Anniversary Treasury*, pp. 311-314).

The wisdom, compassion, and tender mercy of our Father lead Him to do things like that for His children. We call it His "providential" power. Because we believe He can arrange things like that, we confidently pray, "Lead us not into temptation, but deliver us from evil."

His power to deliver us from the evil within us depends on His ability to transform our hearts. He does that by filling us with His Holy Spirit. He teaches us to delight in His way, to set our hearts on things above rather than on the things of this earth.

When we pray, "Thine is the power," we should give ourselves time to meditate on His great power — His creative power, sustaining power, life-giving and life-changing power. Again, make brief notes to remind yourself of the specifics of that power, and in your meditation you will praise Him for creating us in His own image with the ability to reason, to love, to honor and to worship. You will also praise Him for the sustaining power that enables Him to so order time and circumstances that we will be led into the right paths and delivered from evil.

## *THINE IS THE GLORY*

In the third place, Jesus taught us to pray, "Thine is the glory." In so praying, we acknowledge that all glory belongs to Him. Everything that is praiseworthy has its origin and its perfect expression in Him. His very nature, His character is His glory.

Jesus came to earth to show us the character of God. He wanted us to see God as He really is so we would turn to Him in true devotion. He personified all the loveliest virtues: love, tender mercy, gentleness, kindness, compassion, generosity. Peter expressed in very simple terms the kind of life Jesus lived. He said of Him that He "went about doing good" (Acts 10:38).

I suppose there could be no greater illustration of His unsurpassed love than the story of the cross and events leading up to it. The agony of the bitter cup of Gethsemane, the cruel scourging, and the crucifixion itself. Perhaps the most poignant moment of all, tradition tells us it happened as they were raising the cross, at the very moment when His full weight came down on those nails through His hands and feet, He cried out, "Father, forgive them for they know not what they do." Several times during His life men were heard to exclaim, "What manner of man is this?" They asked that when He stilled the storm (Mk. 4:41) and when He cast out demons (Mk. 1:27). I think someone must have asked it then, "What kind of man is this who prays for those who are murdering Him?"

Anyone can say, "I believe He has the power to heal me," but not everyone can trust himself completely to the will of the Lord. Only those who have looked upon His magnificent love, who have come to understand something of His perfect generosity, compassion, gentleness, and tender mercy can say, "Here I am Lord, do with me as You will, for I know Your will is what is best for me. If illness is needed to purify my faith, bring it on. If you must crush me like the petal of a rose to release a fragrant blessing for others, do it Lord. Thy will be done. I say 'Yes' to whatever You want for me, Lord, let it be."

"One day a leper came and knelt in front of Jesus. 'Sir,' he said, 'If you want to, you can make me clean.' Jesus stretched out his hand and placed it on the leper saying, 'Of course I want to. Be clean!', and at once he was clean of leprosy."

That is J.B. Phillips' translation of Matthew 8:2-3. I think he captured the feeling of what happened that day. The leper believed Jesus had the power to heal him, but he didn't understand the compassionate character of our Lord. Of course He wanted to cleanse the man. There is no record of Jesus ever refusing to heal anyone who came to Him asking for healing. He revealed to us God's great, compassionate heart. Only those who have accepted these Bible teachings at face value can turn themselves over completely to His will.

Do you begin to see the great purpose of praise? It is as we continually remind ourselves of God's greatness, His perfect love and mercy — in short, of His goodness — that we learn to trust Him more and more. I urge you to make plenty of time for praise in your personal devotional time. Meditate upon these great facts: All dominion, all power, and all glory belong to Him. His character makes Him totally praiseworthy.

If we want to pray as Jesus taught us to pray, we must take

the time we need to meditate on His greatness and goodness. He taught us to begin and end our prayers with praise. Would you make the commitment with me to be a praying person? Would you:

> Take time to be holy, speak oft with thy Lord
> Abide in Him always and feed on His word.
>
> Take time to be holy, the world rushes on
> Spend much time in secret with Jesus alone.

Would you make that commitment today?

## Discussion Questions

1. Why do you think Jesus taught that praise is an important part of our prayers?

2. Why don't people include praise more often in their public prayers? Do you think people would feel uncomfortable including such phrases as, "Father, You are so wonderful! Your goodness overwhelms me. From everlasting to everlasting You are God. There is no other like You. I will praise Your name forever," in their public prayers?

3. Can you think of an example from your own experience when God used a nonchristian to accomplish His will? What other examples can you give that show God is in control in the affairs of men, even those who don't acknowledge Him?

4. Can you remember a time in your life when God used an ordinary occurrence to change the course of your activities so that they would conform to His will?

5. Can you explain why baptism can not be called a meritorious work? How can God require repentance and baptism (Acts 2:38) before He grants salvation and yet say that we are saved by grace?

6. Three possibilities are discussed of ways to keep your mind focused on your prayers, i.e., writing them, saying them out loud, and writing brief notes and then letting your mind explore all the possibilities. Can you think of other ways to keep your mind from wandering during prayer time?

7. What are some of the ways God's power is demonstrated through our personalities? Our lives?